Maryland Folklore

BY GEORGE G. CAREY

Tidewater Publishers

CENTREVILLE, MARYLAND

Within this work, some of the texts—the specific examples of folk speech, for instance—have been drawn from three of the author's previous, and now no longer available, books: *Maryland Folklore and Folklife*, *Maryland Folk Legends and Folk Songs*, and *A Faraway Time and Place: Lore of the Eastern Shore*.

Library of Congress Cataloging-in-Publication Data

Carey, George Gibson, 1934–
    Maryland folklore / by George G. Carey. — 1st ed.
        p. cm.
    Bibliography: p.
    ISBN 0-87033-396-8 :
    1. Folk literature—Maryland.   2. Maryland—Social
    life and customs.   I. Title.
    GR110.M3C297 1989
    398.2' 09752—dc20   89-40302
                                                   CIP

Manufactured in the United States of America
First edition, 1989; third printing, 1994

Maryland Folklore

Contents

For
Ed and Gary
and in memory of
Captain Alex Kellam

Preface

FOLKLORE has been around in Maryland as long as men and women have been talking to one another between geographical boundaries that define the state as starting here and ending there. Folklorists haven't been around that long, not in a formal sense at any rate. They have only been recognized officially in this country since 1888 when a group of scholars got together in Boston and formed the American Folklore Society. As fate would have it, this same society backed the first attempt to codify Maryland folk traditions when in 1925 they brought out Whitney and Bullock's *Folk-lore from Maryland* as the twenty-eighth volume of their memoir series.

Except for the efforts of Dorothy Howard at Frostburg State College, whose work with children's games received considerable attention, not much by way of folklore activities went on in the state over the next forty-odd years. Then in 1968, Governor Agnew established a commission to study Maryland's folklore and folklife. This commission distributed to members of the state legislature a "guide" of its findings, which in time became my small book, *Maryland Folklore and Folklife*, published by Tidewater Publishers in 1970.

Since that time folklore activities have expanded in the state both on the academic level and in the public sector. Scholars have been abroad in the field producing excellent studies; I refer in particular to Geraldine Johnson's *Weaving Rugs in Maryland* and George McDaniel's *Hearth and Home*, both of which I draw on for material in this book. Beyond these endeavors, folklorists presently offer courses at the University of Maryland, both in College Park and Baltimore County as well as at Salisbury State on the Eastern Shore, and these institutions all have folklore archives that house considerable collectiana.

Outside the academy other individuals have stimulated folklore concerns. In 1974, the Maryland State Arts Council under the visionary directorship of Jim Backas secured seed money from the National Endowment for the Arts to establish the first federally funded state folklorist position in the country. Right now there are more than forty such positions in as many states, but most arts councils call their staff members folk arts coordinators, not state folklorists. I held the post in Maryland for a short time at the outset. In 1976 Charles Camp took over the position and in the past fifteen years he has put together a variety of festivals, programs, films, and the like while at the same time providing funding for a number of folklore projects. The Maryland State Arts Council has continued to offer funding for innovative folklore projects including general operating support for local museums, and in 1988 approved more than a dozen grants for such wide-ranging projects as Jewish photography, maritime folklore, non-western music concerts, oral history in the workplace, and a production of Greek shadow puppet plays.

Things have also been bustling in other areas of the public sector where folklore is concerned. In 1985 Elaine Eff was appointed to the position of city folklorist in Baltimore. She works out of an office on North Avenue where she administers a vital program called Baltimore Traditions. I spent a morning with Elaine not long ago at her place of business, and her energy and enthusiasm are infectious, if a tad exhausting. Twenty minutes into our meeting, listening to what she had been up to in the last two years or so, I felt I needed a nap. Virtually singlehanded she has put together three exhibitions, a documentary photo project, an ethnic resource guide, a series of tours, an impressive publication, three different workshops, and an excellent film on Baltimore screen painters, all done on very limited funding and the goodwill of a great many volunteers.

Equally energetic and capable has been Paula Johnson who, as curator of maritime history and folklore for the Calvert

Marine Museum in Solomons, has worked closely with the watermen's culture in that region. She has compiled a formidable archive of oral history and folklore from men and women whose lives touched the water. She has also been instrumental in mounting several fine displays of watermen's artifacts at the museum, and in 1988 she edited a detailed book, *Working the Water*, which in word and photograph brings to the printed page a telling examination of a certain way of life on the Patuxent River.

When my publisher wrote to ask if I would be interested in updating and combining my two earlier books, *Maryland Folklore and Folklife* and *Maryland Folk Legends and Folk Songs*, I was surprised to learn that the first of these volumes was still in print—just barely, he informed me. I had used the folklore/folklife book periodically in my classes, examining with students ways in which the format could be improved. The ideas my students and I came up with for revamping called for a total restructuring of the text and a vast amount of further fieldwork, tasks I did not feel I had time to carry out. Certainly a different way to write a book about Maryland's folklore and folklife would be to divide the state into geographical regions and ethnic and occupational groups and then show how folklore grows organically from them and what cultural attitudes and values it expresses.

Not given the best of all possible worlds, I have fallen back on the old organizational pattern and set this book once again into the genre format. For texts I have drawn heavily on the folklore/folklife and the legend/folk song books and have incorporated further source material from *A Faraway Time and Place: Lore of the Eastern Shore*, another volume of mine now virtually out of print.

One discrepancy that any student of folklore will notice right away is the lack of any section on folk songs. I justify this seeming oversight in two ways. First, both the folklore/folklife and the legend/folk song books included between them forty songs with annotations (though very few tunes), and it seemed foolish to reprint those songs simply to give this book yet one more genre. Secondly, and more to the point, I believe that traditional singing in Maryland is not what it used to be. That is not to say it is a dead art. Mothers still sing lullabies to their infants, rugby players still bellow the lyrics of obscene songs at beer-drinking fests after their matches. What I mean is that people no longer sit around and listen to long renditions of "Sir Patrick Spens," or "The Brown Girl," or any of a number of the other ballads that appeared in the earlier books—unless it is at a folk song concert. We have ample evidence that these songs and many others like them were sung traditionally at one time in Maryland, but the singers are long since dead and their tradition has unfortunately disappeared with them. On the other hand, I feel that many of the other types of folklore that appear here are still active in certain areas, albeit changed and resuited for a different generation, but nonetheless very much alive. If children no longer sing jump rope rhymes in leaf-strewn playgrounds and local pundits no longer tell stories in favored taverns, then things are out of whack and I have definitely lost my way.

The other thing any observant reader will notice in a hurry is that, though Maryland is reasonably well represented geographically, two regions predominate: the western part of the state around Frostburg, and the lower Eastern Shore of Chesapeake Bay. The reason for this is simple enough. Dorothy Howard taught folklore at Frostburg State College for a good many years and back in the late 1960s she was good enough to pass on to me much of the material she and her students had gathered over the years. My own fieldwork, also back in the late sixties and early seventies, took me to the watermen's culture around Crisfield and the off-lying islands, Smith and Tangier, where I encountered a vigorous storytelling tradition. The remaining material in this book comes from student collections now housed in an archive at the University of Maryland in College Park.

With an eye to the recent developments in folklife studies, I have completely redone the material culture section that appeared in the folklore/folklife volume, introducing for the most part all new materials. To be sure, my efforts are very much at surface level, but they may give some indication to others interested in this sort of thing, what incredible potential for study the state of Maryland provides.

A final note to the general reader. He or she may justifiably wonder why I chose to quote so many storytelling texts and not to simply rewrite the tales in a more literate form. Since folklore is primarily passed on by word of mouth, it seems only fair to the tellers of these tales to recount them in the very words in which they were originally rendered. If the grammar and syntax fall a bit out of line, so what; that is the way people speak and God bless them for it. The printed page will never recapture the wonderful flight of a well-told oral narrative with all its voice inflections, gestures, and facial expressions, but the least I can do is to retain the actual words in which these stories were told and that is just what I have done.

No endeavor like this, even the relatively simple revision of older materials, gets done without the gracious help and advice of others. Going way back I can thank the English Department at the University of Maryland which, along with the American Council for Learned Societies and the American Philosophical Society, furnished financial aid for my early field studies. Looking astern to people who helped me early on, I think of Esther Birdsall, Richard Dorson, Henry Glassie, Joe Hickerson, Ray Korson, Ellen Paul, and George Simpson. More recently a clutch of other individuals have aided me in my pursuits. Paul Foer gave me a place to stay in Annapolis while I was there, and kept me amused with his dreadful puns. Charlie Camp furnished a number of good leads and suggestions, and so did Geraldine Johnson. Elaine Eff, Paula Johnson, and Geraldine Johnson were kind enough to supply me with information and photographs for the material culture chapter. I am also grateful to Gerry Parsons of the Archive of Folk Culture at the Library of Congress who in his quiet unassuming way probably knows more about Maryland folkways than anyone around. If Gerry ever gets around to writing a book on Maryland folklife, I daresay it will far outstrip this one.

Finally, there have been a good many people "out there" in the state of Maryland who have given freely of their time while a folklorist sat by with a tape recorder or notebook and gathered what they had to say. Many of them don't get named here, but they know who they are and I hope they will recognize their riddles or proverbs or stories. I want them to know that I am very grateful for what they had to tell. When you come right down to it, this is much more *their* book than it is mine.

I suppose it is also conventional—and perhaps wise—to thank one's wife in such matters as these. So I'll do that—just to be on the safe side.

Maryland Folklore

Introduction

HOW MANY TIMES have you heard someone say, "Come on now, that's nothing but folklore," just after someone else has uttered a suspect truth? I've heard it often enough, God knows, and it never really bothered me much until I became a folklorist. Now when I hear it, my innards seize up tight and I interpret it as yet one more individual setting all folklore aside as nothing more than a pack of lies.

Folklore is not all lies, believe me. Yet I would not say that every bit of folklore clings tightly to absolute fact either. A book of fairy tales or a collection of tall tales can't be set on the same library shelf as sound documented history. Just for discussion's sake, let's take a look at a well-known proverb, "A stitch in time saves nine." I confess I know virtually nothing about knitting and purling, but my wife, who does, tells me that it's true, if you miss a stitch, the stitches below that one may unravel and if you don't notice it in time you're in severe trouble. One thing I do know something about is the metaphorical underpinnings of this proverb. When it comes to mechanical things I'm a complete dolt. If you want someone to rewire a lamp fixture so it will never light again or reset a cooling system so the engine explodes, I'm your man. I know an awful lot about those unsaved stitches, having been one who forever has had to back off on a job and begin all over again. In fact, I think if I had saved up all the time I've lost when I've metaphorically missed a stitch, I'd have half a lifetime to live over again. As irritating as this little fact is to recall, I know folklore in this case holds more truth than I would care to admit.

The truth of the subject aside, we do know that ever since the term *folklore* was coined back in 1846 by the Englishman

3

William Thoms, scholars have been squabbling over its defini-
tion. A lot of what they have argued about would be pretty
tedious for most readers. If you don't believe me simply skim
through the twenty-one definitions listed in the *Standard Dictionary of Folklore, Mythology and Legend,* and you'll find that
even the so-called experts are a long way from agreement on
what folklore embraces.

I have no intention of getting bogged down here over how
many demons can dance on top of a tenpenny nail. Rather I
prefer to run in danger's way by being simplistic, and perhaps
the best way to do that is to clear up some of the common mis-
conceptions about folklore. One of those is that folklore has to
be old, that it has to stem from some hoary past. The fact is that
people are unconsciously passing folklore along this very moment in the speech they use, the jokes they tell, the clothes they
wear, the way they spend their morning, and these activities
have of late become very much part of what folklorists study.
Beyond this, many people feel that folklore has to be rurally
connected. The image of the old codger sitting on the back
stoop swilling corn liquor and mouthing old yarns is a hard
one to shake. And I grant you, a good deal of folklore does
issue from isolated rural areas. In fact, much of what appears in
this book stems from pockets of culture that are hardly urban.
Yet that is not to say that a city like Baltimore does not hold
equally rich pockets of culture within its ethnic neighborhoods;
a folklorist could easily spend three lifetimes in that city with a
battalion of fieldworkers and there would be plenty left to do
when they finished.

"Beware the adjectives 'charming' and 'delightful' when
applied to folktales and folksongs," wrote Richard Dorson.
And admittedly there is good reason to think of much of
folklore that way. We could certainly label quaint or cute such
things as autograph book verse, children's rhymes and games,
riddles, and certain customs. But folklore has another side to be
found in the gnarled grammar or torn phrase of the folk idiom,
the ruptured syntax of folk speech, the rich obscenity of a dirty
joke, the scatological lyrics of a raunchy song. These seeming
aberrations also make a folklorist's antennae bend to and fro.

Finally there is the tendency of a great many people to associate folklore with fabricated heroes, and here I have in mind the figure of Paul Bunyan. There is only the slightest evidence from oral tradition that Bunyan was ever a real folk hero among loggers. When the country emerged from World War I, America simply required some kind of grass roots hero, and Paul Bunyan filled that need. So far as we know, Bunyan was actually the creation of an advertising agent for a California-based logging company. Nonetheless, his popularity spawned a number of what Richard Dorson termed "fakelore" heroes like Annie Christmas, Joe Magarac, and Old Stormalong—each one representing a specific American occupation. They, too, issued from the imaginations of hack writers and journalists. What I hope this book shows among other things is that a real folk hero can exist in story or legend at the local level, merely at the recall of a neighborhood raconteur.

Who then are the folk, and what is their lore? Modern folklorists contend that a folk group is any group of people who have at least one thing in common. It might be occupation, language, religion, ethnicity, or geographical isolation. One can see quite readily how a group of people living beyond or at the edge of what we might call "the main stream" would have a tendency to hang onto their traditional ways since popular culture does not infiltrate a remote area all that easily. It is quite obvious though that in this country these really remote areas have become less so as highway systems have opened up the back country and television has become a primary home appliance.

Clearly the smallest folk unit would be the family, and one could turn there at any time to see folklore and folk tradition at work in microcosm. Who is designated family historian and keeper of the traditions? Who tells the stories at the family gatherings? How are the holidays celebrated? Who cooks? What is served? What nicknames get pinned on family members? All these questions a folklorist might turn inward on his or her own family to better understand how the folk process works and what traditional glues bind the family together and give it its own identity. But the average person moves well beyond the family in a lifetime, coursing among other groups at school, in the workplace, in pastimes or hobbies, in summer recreations, and consequently comes into contact with a variety of lore.

With the lore itself, folklorist Alan Dundes has given a sensible list pointing out that not all folklore can be labeled "in oral tradition." Some forms like gestures, he notes, are not passed along by word of mouth, but rather by imitation. Conversely, graffiti and autograph book verse are actually drawn or written. Other forms get cranked out on the mimeograph or copy machine. To give some notion of folklore's wide-ranging eclecticism, I select from Dundes' list. Folklore includes myths, legends, folktales, jokes, proverbs, riddles, chants, curses, oaths, tongue twisters, folk drama, folk belief, folk medicine, folk song, folk instrumental music, folk speech, children's games, counting-out and jump rope rhymes, nicknames, and place names. It also embraces prayers (for example, graces), gestures, symbols, quilt designs, street vendors' cries, mnemonic devices, barn and fence types, festivals, and holiday customs.

One thing folklore must display is adaptability and change. If something appears over and over again in absolutely the same style or shape it is probably not folklore. A split rail fence on the other hand is very seldom made the same way by two different builders; nor does a dead-rise workboat on the shore of the Potomac River ever turn out exactly the same way twice, though its basic form can be clearly discerned. Likewise, jokes get altered depending on teller and audience, and a singer will take a folk song and make it very much his own though it is still quite recognizable as a version of "The Wreck of the Old '97."

Possibly the best way to witness such variation is to take a well-known tale told on the Eastern Shore of Maryland (and all over the eastern seaboard for that matter) and see just what different storytellers do with it. I began to hear this story as soon as I started collecting folktales down in the Crisfield region and several people who told me the story said they had heard it from an old man named Fletcher Cox. Curious to seek out a source, I took my tape recorder over to Cox's place one sultry afternoon, and he spun me this yarn.

Now, my grandfather, old man Michael Sommers, he had made his money when navigators were scarce. At that time, one hundred years ago, a good navigator could go all over the world. And then they were going in square riggers; no steamships then. And at that time a navigator could take a ship anywhere in the world, and they made good money. And they made runs to China and Japan and all around the South Sea islands, and after he retired from doing that, he had a store on Old Island, Jane's Island they called it, and he built a store on that. And at that time there were no roads out there and people went there by boat. And all up and around Fairmount and Deal Island there wasn't any store worth a damn, so they'd come down there to the island by boat. It was a lot quicker than going on an old cart road with a horse, riding. And he had this big store, and all the dredge boats they'd come in there and anchor at night.

Well, while he was at the store, he started a school and he had about ten fellows and he taught them navigation. And he had two fellows from Crisfield, Captain Len Tawes and Captain Ben Tawes, and then he had some other guy by the name of Culver. Then he had a lot from around Virginia. They come up there and took navigation from him.

Now the yarn they used to tell about that, it was Len Tawes told this a long time ago, and he said it was the truth and he wasn't exaggerating it. So Captain Len said that Captain Michael got them out there on the Bay, out of sight of land and he said, "Come on boys, take the sun and your latitude and tell me where you're at." And so they did and he said, "I think you boys are O.K. and I can turn you loose and you can go anywhere you want." And so he give them their papers.

So he said they went to Baltimore and they figured they could get a ship. They'd both go, one would go as captain and the other as mate. So when they got to Baltimore, there was this fellow Langhammer; he was a big fruit buyer and he owned ships. And he run down to the West Indies and South America and he didn't go across, but he run fruit mostly for the West Indies. And so they went to Langhammer to see if they could get a ship. And they showed him their papers, you know. Well, Langhammer said, "I know Michael wouldn't have sent you if you weren't right, but you're young, you're young. I got a brand new boat that just come off the ways and I'd like for you guys to go as mate or something like that for two or three trips until you know more about it." But they kept after him to let them have the boat, so finally he said, "I tell you what I'm going to do: You're young and you've never been to sea, but if you can get hold of old Michael to make one trip with you I'll let you have the boat."

Well Captain Len he said they got in the canoe in Baltimore and came on back to Old Island and came in there and old man Michael said, "How did you make out?"

"Well, we went to Langhammer and he told us the only way he'd let us have the boat was for you to make a trip with us. Go to the West Indies and load fruit."

Michael said, "Well, I'm retired, I can't go to sea anymore. I've got this store and I'm teaching and it's really impossible. But," he said, "if I can get old man Hance Lawson to take the store, I'll make the trip."

"Well," they said, "you'll have to give us the papers to take back to Langhammer."

Old man Michael gave him [sic] the papers and told Lang-hammer to let them have the boat, and they come on down the Bay to Old Island and they picked him up and he made the trip with them.

And they went on out and Michael said, "O.K. boys, take your sun and get your courses and all and let me look at them." So they did and they were all right and they had a good trip and they got to the West Indies and they loaded with fruit. And they said there were a lot more boats laying loading fruit, come from Baltimore and New York and different places. And there were two of Langhammer's boats loading there. And after they got loaded, they all put out practically together, and old man Michael stayed down in the cabin most of the time. And he said, "Send your chart down to me and your log and let me read that. You're doing all right."

Well, just before they got to the Bay, it set in foggy and you couldn't see a thing. All them boats they got inside of Cape Henry on the anchoring ground and they anchored. Didn't want to start up the Bay—no buoys in the Bay or nothing. And they couldn't see a thing. But old man Michael he said, "We're going up the Bay; this fog is going to last three days and they're going to lose their fruit. We're going up the Bay and our fruit will be in good shape."

Now after they got by Old Point he said, "Boys, get me your lead line and bring me down a sample from the bottom." And there was just enough light breeze a-going and they were going right up the Bay. "Bring me down a sounding every half hour, twenty minutes would be better, but don't make it over half an hour before you bring me down another sample."

He went back down there in the cabin. They throwed the lead line over and it come up about several handfuls of mud and they passed it down to him and he looked at it and he said, "All right, boys, you're doing all right, but change your course about three or four points to the westward and that will put you right in the middle of the channel in the next half hour."

Well, they done that and come the night and the fog was so thick they said you had to feel the man that was next to you. And they were steering with a light over the compass they could see that, and this fellow Ward says, "Uncle, he doesn't know where we are. We're going to run this boat aground and we'll never get another one. Langhammer nor nobody else will ever give us another boat. He don't know where he's at, foggy as it is."

Well, Captain Len said, "We ain't run ashore yet, and every time you've thrown the line you've had some water."

So he carried a sample down and he come back up on deck and Uncle Michael said, "Now hold right on that course for the next half hour."

So they talked and Ward said, "Damned if I ain't going to find out what you know."

His mother was a great flower arranger and she lived right here to what they call Ward's Crossing and she had the best flower garden in Somerset County. Her name was Betsy Ann Ward. And she knowed she'd never get to see him no more and she give him a flower in a pot to take aboard and remember her by. And so he said, "Len, I'm going to see how much he knows; you know that flower that mother gave me and brought on board? I'm going to throw that flower overboard and I'm going to wet that dirt from overboard and put it in there and send it down to him."

9

(It's the truth. I've heard them both tell it. Course Captain Ward got drownded, but Captain Len lived to be an old man, and I've heard him tell it a hundred times.)

He put this in there, dipped the lead line overboard and he dumped it out on the platter and sent it down to the old man. And he mushed it like mud, you know. Well, Michael said, "Seems to me we're going all right." And he looked at this, looked all around, went through it and says, "Henry, run up just as quick as you can and tell Len to heave her hard to. You're right in the middle of Betsy Ann's flower garden."

Cox's marvelously detailed account gives us names of places and people and even suggests dates since we know when some of the characters in it lived. What we discover, however, is that the tale did not originate with Cox, but with Captain Len Tawes. Yet we know it didn't really begin with Tawes either, and though he evidently told it on himself and close friends, the story in one form or other has doubtless been around since seafarers have been sounding the bottom with a lead line. What is curious from the folklorist's viewpoint is how different raconteurs handle the tale. As the story gets removed from its source it begins to lose some of its detail. And at the hands of more modern storytellers, the tale becomes much less a yarn, much more an anecdote. Older storytellers seem to luxuriate in the time it takes to tell their tale, while their modern counterparts, more comfortable with the joke, just want to get the job done.

For instance, an older man named Simmon Tilghman said he had heard the story from Cox, and in his version there is little deviation from Cox's story, only the character of Langhammer in Baltimore has dropped out, and the flower garden belongs to Sarey Ann, not Betsy Ann Ward. But in the account of William Murray from Mount Vernon, a lot of information has dropped away and the whole tale has shifted a generation with Tawes now in the old navigator's role.

There's a man down to Crisfield named Fletcher Cox told me this story. I don't know if it's true or what, but it's supposed to be connected with Captain Tawes who was a great commercial waterman. He had several ships and after he got through following the water he run a store, and he didn't have any cash registers. He just kept his money in nail kegs and they just had half-dollars in those days and all he sold was stuff to go with the waterman's needs such as oilskins and gum boots and crab nets and whatnot. And after he kept store for a number of years he got so old and he couldn't move out so he started up a navigation school up above the store and he taught people down there to Crisfield how to sail ships.

So one year in particular there were these two boys and they wanted to go to Baltimore to get a ship. So they went to Baltimore and there wasn't nothing but one ship available, and that ship was a small sailing vessel and the man wouldn't turn it over to them unless they could get Captain Tawes to make one initial trip with them. And so they came back to Crisfield from Baltimore and told Captain Tawes that the man wouldn't let them have the vessel unless he would make the first trip. So finally he agreed, and they went to Porta Rica and loaded with fruit, oranges and bananas and grapefruit, and they started back from Porta Rica and they got into the Capes and there came an awful calm and these vessels anchored except for this one man and he said, "Well, we have to keep her going or these people are going to lose their fruit."

So they kept her going up the Bay and every once in a while there was a thick fog, and every once in a while he asked for the lead line and they'd throw a lead line out and the Captain would read it. He never got out of the cabin he was so old, and they carried the lead line down to him and he read it.

And after a time these boys got scared and they thought they were going to run ashore and lose all their cargo, so they said to themselves, "We'll find out what he knows."

So when the next time came when they threw out the lead line, they took some dirt from a flower pot that the old Captain's wife had sent along (she thought he might never come back so she sent some flower pots along for the trip). So they took some dirt out of the flower pot and put it on the lead line and brought it down to the old man and said, "Where are we now?"

He felt that, looked it all over, and he said, "Well, I'll tell you,

11

I'm not sure, but I think we're in the midst of old Betsy's flower garden."

In a rendition by Alex Kellam, a storyteller who by his own admission liked short humorous tales, all the original characters have dropped away and his account becomes an anecdote told on a local character.

I think his name was Ben Fudge. Benjamin Evans, but they called him Ben Fudge. Not knowing navigation (I don't suspect his was all memory), but they said they were going to Baltimore on this trip and said they would take their chickens right aboard and their geese and have them whenever they needed them, wanted them. And so he was telling them that he could tell exactly where they were by the smell of the mud from the lead line. So they started off and when they got off Bear's Island, they dropped the lead line.

He said, "You're right off Holland's Bar, about twenty miles off of here."

They said, "Damn it, right."

So they went up there till they got off Barren Island, and they took another sounding. He said, "Right off Hooper's Strait, right off on Barren Island Light."

On up the Bay about eight or ten times and finally one of them said, "Damn, if we don't see what the hell he does this time." So one of them took that lead line and smeared it around in the chicken coop, you know.

"'Bout time for another sounding."

So they passed the lead down to him and he took it. "Goddamn, if I didn't know we were right off of Thomas Point, I swear I was right home in the backyard."

In Kellam's version the story has started its drift towards a scatological tale. Rob Williams's account moves it further in that direction with yet another character in the lead role.

This sailboat captain, his name was Richard Fenn, and he hired two fellows to go to Baltimore with him. He was a good captain, no booze, didn't want no booze on the boat. You had to know the water. They said, "We're going to fool him."

(You've heard of lead lines, ain't you? Well, you know they got a little hole in the center and then you get the smell of it and from the bottom you can tell where you're at.) They went out to his grandmother's I think it was to the toilet and dropped it down in the hole and they carried it aboard with them.

Well, they were going up the Bay and he said, "Boys, where we at?"

They said, "We don't know."

He said, "Sound the bottom, let's smell of it."

Well, they out with the lead line dropped it down that toilet, they found the bottom; he smelled of it and said, "Lookee here, if you don't get this boat about, damned if we ain't going to run aground on a shithouse."

Finally, in a version told me by Dewey Landon there are none of the original touchstones, no place, no people, just the framework of a story whose central purpose seems to be the scatological punch line.

They claim there was an old captain going up and down the Bay here, and no matter what, he could taste the bottom and tell you where you was at. He done it so much, he knew the different tastes of the bottom. And one of them he went and dumped, and he shoved the lead line down in it and went and [the Captain] tasted it and said, "I'll tell you one thing, if we don't get this boat turned around, we're going to run into a shithouse."

Whether or not we could do the same kind of examination for every item of folklore that appears in this book would be hard to say. Certainly for the shorter forms like the proverb and the riddle, there is much less room for alteration. Still, in all folklore we see the process of change at work, each storyteller sifting and shifting his material to make it fit his own needs. At times a narrator will draw on small elements of folklore (folklorists call them folk motifs) and subconsciously insert them into the framework of a story. Here, for example, is a splendid bit of family oral history told to me by Captain Otis Evans of Crisfield in 1968:

My uncle told me this happened to my great-great-grand-father, and I suppose it's true. His name was William Evans and he was living on the Bay at Smith Island, and at that time Smith Island was sparsely settled. They were scattered from Kedges Strait to Tangiers. The old man had a farm and a herd of cattle and he thought enough of them as if they'd been Aberdeen Angus. But they were hide and horn mostly.

When the British left Baltimore after they got whipped [in 1814] they were becalmed off Smith Island and their provisions were about gone. They looked over through their binoculars and they could tell there were cattle roaming around on the beach. So when the old man got up this morning, he looked down there and there was a longboat on the Bay shore and a bunch of bluecoats there around his cattle. Well, he saw the fire right away, so he grabbed his old walking stick and he got down there to the beach and he started waving that thing around, you know; so those men gathered him up, tied him and put him in the longboat, and took him aboard the boat.

Now this all happened when tobacco-chewing come in. The old man was a great chewer—grew his own tobacco. So he sat there in the main cabin of the ship chewing his tobacco. But he didn't know where to spit. Oh, they had a plush carpet you could sink into. So by and by he found himself a corner and he spit into it. Here comes a little fella dressed up in white and he put down a big silver-looking thing, all bright and shiny. So after a little while the old man had to spit again, he looked around—couldn't spit in that beautiful thing—so he found himself another corner and let loose. And that fella run and grabbed that silver thing and put it in this corner. So it finally got on the old man's nerves and he said, "If you don't take that *dahmn* thing out of my way, I'll spit right into it."

"Oh, Captain Evans, that's just what we want you to do."

"Well," he says, "good enough." So he sat there. Said he had the greatest evening of his life. But later on it breezed up, so they went on down to Tangiers, 'cause they had a deepwater harbor there. They went there for repairs before they went back to England. And they told Captain Evans—he'd been as contrary as he could be—"Mr. Evans, we're going to take you back to England."

He said, "That's just what I want you to do, take me back to England. I want to tell the *dahmn* queen just what a bunch of cutthroats she sent over here, anyhow. You're no good."

(And according to my uncle, my grandparents did hate the British. Oh yes, they called them *dahmn* Britishers, and they weren't cussing people as a rule. They were church-abiding men, but they used the term *dahmn* Britishers.) But anyhow, the day came that the British were all ready to sail back to England, and so they changed their mind on grandpap. They said, "Mr. Evans, you're too brave a man to keep in custody. We're going to send you back home."

And so the man in charge put an officer over him and said, "You take Mr. Evans back to Smith Island and you be sure to put him on dry land." So they got up there to Horse Hammock, the tide was down low and there was this sandbar going out there for one hundred yards or more from the shore. They said, "Mr. Evans, you'll have to walk from here. This is as close as we can get."

He said, "I heard your commanding officer tell you: Put me on dry land. And you'd better do it or there's going to be trouble. I'll report you, certain." So the four of them picked him up, one ahold of each arm and they carried him ashore and set him down on the grass. "Now," he said, "you can go."

Otis Evans is dealing here with history which stretches back more than a century and a half. How accurate his account is, is something that would be very difficult to determine as there is little of written record that documents the history of Smith or Tangier Island. Yet the tale seems more a way of demonstrating not just the eccentricities of Evans's great-great-grandfather, but also the strident patriotism among these early islanders. What the folklorist notices stuck away in the middle of this run of oral history is the well-known folktale about the spittoon. The same tale was told on Davy Crockett when he went to Washington, and it has doubtless been hung on many other backwoods tobacco chewers. Yet had I pointed this out to Captain Evans, he would have probably responded, "But that's the way I always heard it." Besides, pointing this fact out to him would have served no purpose whatsoever.

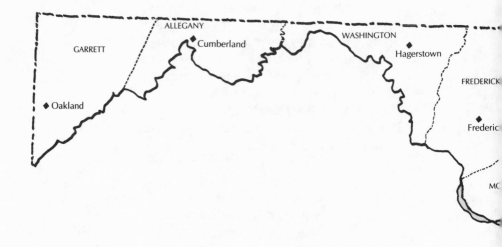

Maryland

Counties and County Seats

The folklorist's job is simply to collect his data, organize it, and then evaluate and analyze it to the best of his ability. Unless he is collecting within his own family, the folklorist will usually be an outsider and his presence will sometimes disconnect the normal set and continuity of life. But if he is aware of that, if he is sensitive to the community where he is working, honest and compassionate towards his informants, and sincere in his motive about observing cultural phenomena, then his results will become beneficial to both his discipline and the people he is studying.

1. Folktales and Tall Tales

STORYTELLING AND STORYTELLERS

ORAL STORYTELLERS have been around a lot longer than novelists. We have every reason to believe that such epic works as the *Odyssey* and parts of the Bible were at one time long accounts which were passed on by word of mouth, the only means at that time of preserving history. Someone at some point simply had the wisdom to write them down.

Obviously, the art of modern storytelling differs considerably from what it was back in Homer's time. In many places today, in fact, storytelling is quite different from what it was even two or three generations ago. We no longer seem to have the time to sit around and enjoy a long elaborate narrative. We are too busy, and thus the quick opening joke with its punch line as cinch has replaced the delightful entanglements of the tall tale or the intricate ramifications of the fairy tale.

Then, too, there is the intrusion of television. Probably no other single thing has done more to diminish the oral storyteller's art than this medium. Older people in the small communities on the lower Eastern Shore of Maryland remember how they used to gather evening upon evening at the local store to spin yarns and get the local news. Now they sit home in front of the television in a much more passive frame of mind, and the store, that once vital forum for village communication, closes up early.

In practically every folk group or community one can usually find what the folklorist calls an "active bearer" of tradition. He or she is that person who is touted as "the guy who sings all those dirty songs" or "the fellow who knows a lot of

19

the old stories they used to tell around here." On the back side of this coin are—once more in the folklorist's jargon—the "passive bearers," those individuals who are familiar with the local traditions but do not feel actively compelled to perform them. Passive bearers usually compose the audience.

If one thinks again for a moment of that smallest of all folk units, their family, I'm sure he or she can recall someone who at family gatherings is always called upon to perform, be it with family history, old songs, jokes, or traditional toasts. These active bearers, aware of their own reputations and the likelihood that they will be requested either to entertain or inform, consciously add to their repertoire of material.

If we move out from the family to another context, namely the nonliterate society where oral tradition predominates, we see just how important this active tradition bearer is. We think here of the Irish shanackie, or in African cultures, the griot or the alcalla. In these tightly knit societies, the griot and the shanackie become the repository for all the lore and history that the group holds dear. (Griot, loosely translated, means "speaking document.") In time, the griot passes this body of information on to an appointed younger person.

Obviously, no such conscious line of oral transmission takes place in Maryland communities. But that is not to say that these communities do not have their own active bearers. The most remarkable one I ever encountered was Captain Alex Kellam, an ex-waterman turned insurance salesman, and I met him, appropriately enough, on the "liar's bench" at the waterfront in Crisfield. Prior to our introduction, he had been described to me by other local people as "someone who can really tell you something." And at our first meeting I was hardly disappointed. He walked out onto the dock dressed in a coat, a hat, and a tie, and immediately began telling stories as I feverishly jotted down the gist of them in my notebook.

Kellam grew up on Smith Island and never went beyond the eighth grade in school. Instead, like so many others in these offshore communities, he set out to follow the water dredging oysters aboard the *Ruby Ford* over in the Potomac River. Later he married the girl who had come out to teach school on Smith

Island, and they moved ashore to Crisfield. After a number of years on the water, Kellam began selling life insurance for a firm in Salisbury.

Even in his late years Kellam was always the picture of health. As a youth he had done some amateur boxing, something he was quite proud of, and over the years he had kept in shape, never let his powerful frame get "pussy," as the local people phrased it. Out of Kellam's barrel chest rolled a resonant baritone voice filled with laughter and surprise and tempered to amuse even the most solemn listener. "I guess the greatest compliment I ever got," he announced one day, "was when this fellow told me, 'Kellam, even when you're feeling bad, you can still make people laugh.'"

But Kellam also had the one thing an active bearer needs above all—a good memory. He recounted how as a young boy he used to hang around the local store at Rhodes Point on Smith Island just to listen to the "old head" talk. "It was sort of a hobby with me," he explained, "remembering all those stories I used to hear, and I haven't forgotten many of them even now."

In retirement, Kellam had a good deal of free time. He spent it hanging around the local Crisfield watering holes or down at wharfside where the ferries from Smith and Tangier Island came and went. Summers he worked part time at a state run campsite north of Crisfield where campers soon recognized him as a delightful source of local knowledge and information. One thing Kellam never lacked for was an audience.

As a storyteller Kellam provided a good deal of narrative drama. He often acted out his stories with facial grimaces, hand gestures, dialectical innovations, onomatopoetic sounds, voice alterations. He laced his yarns with jingles and rhymes, and would from time to time break into song. (He had a fine voice, having sung with a local barbershop quartet.) His stories fairly bristled with places and names of old characters, many long since dead, but in Kellam's recountings they came to life with a passionate flair which made their idiosyncrasies seem as believable as they were amusing.

Kellam preferred the short anecdotal story, one which in-

21

variably had a punch line to top it off. He once confessed to me his distaste for storytellers who edged with their narratives and failed to come to the point quickly. Kellam easily combined the jokes he had picked up at the office in Salisbury with the stories he remembered from Smith Island, though he obviously liked the older stories better for they had a more polished quality from constant retelling.

Kellam never seemed ill at ease whether he was talking to a classroom of Yale undergraduates (as he did when I taught a course at that university in 1982) or speaking in a large lecture hall. But he was obviously most comfortable and at his tale-telling best when wandering about the waterfront in Crisfield. In a clutch of old watermen whose memories and anecdotes stimulated his own, he at once became the center of attention, the performer, the master raconteur.

At the end of his life Kellam gained a certain visibility that made him somewhat of a celebrity. In 1976 he had been the cornerstone of a film on Maryland folklife done by the public broadcasting people in Owings Mills. He also became a popular after dinner speaker well beyond Somerset County. But the theme of all his talks was always his cultural roots on the Eastern Shore. When he died in 1986 at the age of seventy-eight in a car accident, Kellam had just appeared on the pages of *People* magazine and become part of a weekly television show in Salisbury.

In April I flew down to his funeral. I remember the evening before the service I stood in the funeral parlor with the director. Kellam's casket lay against the wall on the other side of the room. Our conversation about the man wound down. The director nodded toward the casket. "I'll tell you one thing," he said, "the Eastern Shore has certainly lost a great friend in that man."

Quite different from Kellam yet no less appreciated in his community was another waterman named George Alan Wheatley. Wheatley spent his very early years in Maryland on the western shore of Chesapeake Bay, moving out to Tangier Island as a young boy. When I met him in the late 1960s he was ninety-two, not only the oldest man on the island, but obviously the one the local people recognized as the source of island history and tradition. After he moved to Tangier, he followed the only occupation available.

> I started right out on the water. I've drudged on California Rock with cranks for twenty-five cents a day, eight dollars a month . . . Well, when I got married, that was in '98, I weren't getting but thirty-five dollars a month, and I married a woman with two children. In 1903 I bought me my own bateau, that's what they called them then, bateaux, and I got ready and got some men together and we went to Richmond to get some niggers to go dredging. We took out a third for the boat and all hands shared equal what was left. And the most money I've ever got for a bushel of oysters, and I've seen many a one, was a dollar and thirty-five cents.

Wheatley's style and repertoire differed markedly from Kellam's. The quick opening joke was conspicuously missing. Wheatley mixed into his arsenal of stories belief tales, legends, oral history, and tall tales. His recall gave his listeners a window into the nineteenth century, for what he recounted in large part was what he remembered hearing from older watermen when he was a younger man. From this old man's deft recall for places, people, and events, a listener could easily piece together a montage of the waterman's way of life as it existed one hundred years ago. Harbors and oystering rocks appeared in the minutest detail; gales and tides and memorable catches and hard times on the water came to Wheatley's mind with the precision of a document.

Yet there was in Wheatley's delivery a rote quality that Kellam seldom displayed. It was obvious that he had been asked to tell these stories many times before and over the years he had honed them to an almost mechanical fidelity. If you asked him for strong man stories, he obliged with a whole cycle of tales told almost word for word each time about a character named George Davey. Wheatley formulas for tales seemed fixed, his rhythms downbeat. He achieved his emphasis not so much by verbal fireworks as by simply engaging his audience

23

with his eyes, leaning forward in his chair, and almost physically thrusting home the point of his yarn.

In the early stages of any project the folklorist's job is to seek out and find storytellers like Kellam and Wheatley, that is, if he or she is looking for oral narratives. Once the material has been gathered and codified into some sort of workable form, then the folklorist's job is to examine what he has found and see just what it means. Stories get told over and over in a community or among a group of people for a reason, though the group itself may not be aware of exactly what that reason is. If we look closely at almost any story we begin to see certain things that tell us something about the values and attitudes that motivate a way of life. Take for example this story of Alex Kellam's:

> This man, Captain Sam, they called him, lived up there to the Nanticoke River near Mount Vernon. He handled his oysters pretty rough and he knew the law was going to get him sooner or later. Well, he had this colored man working with him, you know. So this one morning, there was this inspector in a rowboat trying to sneak up on him. Well, Sam saw him and he turned to the nigger and he said, "John, shovel them oysters up on the end of this culling board." He had maybe two or three bushels. John shoveled them right up there and got them all ready. Well, the inspector inched his way to a place where he thought he had him and he come a-rowing as hard as he could, and when he come up alongside, Captain Sam and John upended that culling board and ccuuussshhh, them oysters went right back overboard. That inspector looked right at him and said, "Sam, what in the hell are you doing?"
>
> Sam said, "Fulfilling the scriptures."
>
> Inspector said, "Fulfilling the scriptures, what do you mean?"
>
> He said, "Well, you know what the scriptures say, 'Be ye ever so ready for you know not the moment or the hour when the son-of-a-bitch cometh.'"

For those unfamiliar with the waterman's way, what is happening here is that Captain Sam has the reputation for taking oysters that may be under the legal limit, but rather than face the humiliation of undergoing a check by an authority figure he has no respect for, he opts to dump his entire morning's work back into the Bay. More to the waterman's delight though is the way Sam makes a fool out of the inspector. On the Eastern Shore there are probably no people who suffer more verbal (and sometimes physical) abuse than the game wardens and the marine police inspectors. To local fishermen these agents in their green uniforms and yellow shoulder patches poking around in piles of oysters or crab catches stand for all that is bad about Annapolis and government restrictions. The waterman sees his own freedoms as fragile enough and he firmly believes he does not need a further check on what William Warner has called his "right of free plunder."

It is Captain Sam's style and method of demeaning the inspector that would appeal to any local person listening to this tale on the waterfront. In a good Methodist community like the lower Eastern Shore, one's ability to quote the scriptures is admired. The witty retort is also admired, and here Captain Sam has used them both very effectively to exorcise one of the waterman's worst demons. It is not hard to see why a tale like this would linger on the Eastern Shore. Anyone who follows the water can identify with this situation and these characters. What is more, the good guy, even though he loses his catch, wins the day and the bad guy looks very foolish.

FOLK NARRATIVES

Folktales appear in any of a number of guises in Maryland from the complexities of the fairy tale and the cumulative tale to the simplest joke. What becomes quickly clear to anyone collecting folktales is that the storytellers themselves seldom make any distinction between the kind of story they tell, just as a traditional folk singer will not differentiate between an old ballad learned from a grandmother and a song picked up the week before on the radio from the Grand Ole Opry. They are simply good stories or songs worth telling or singing, and the process of classification is left to the folklorist.

Another thing the folklorist discovers in collecting stories today is that most of the tale telling is anecdotal. Only occasionally does one stumble across the märchen or fairy tale, and even when one does it is usually in a relatively truncated form. For example this version of "Cinderella" collected in Salisbury in the late 1960s:

Lady had two daughters and adopted Cinderella. That made three. So the king had a big dance that night and at that dance the king was supposed to find a wife. The king had one gold slipper and whichever lady that slipper fit, that would be the king's wife.

So this lady dressed her two daughters the best she could in pearls and diamonds because she knew her daughters would look beautiful and put poor Cinderella in the dutch oven and locked her in.

As the king asked for a dance with the slipper in his hand, whoever he danced with was supposed to fit the slipper to her feet. So the lady said, "Mr. King, here are my two beautiful daughters. I know it will fit either one, so take my daughter to be your wife."

So the king tried the slipper on both girls' feet and neither one could wear it. So he said, "Madame, dear lady, I'm sorry. Neither one of your daughters can be my wife because they cannot wear my golden shoes."

And at that time Cinderella began to sing in the oven: "You can repair your feet, you can cut off your toe, but the owner of that slipper is in this oven."

So the king said, "Madame, I heard somebody singing, may I see the lady singing?"

She said, "Oh, Mr. King, don't listen to that dirty little girl. She's just a nuisance when good men come around. My daughter is the girl to wear that golden slipper."

The king said, "How can that be when it doesn't fit her foot?"

The lady said, "Oh, Mr. King, we can cut off the toes so it will fit. She must be your wife."

The king said, "Madame, it just wouldn't work."

At that moment, poor Cinderella began to sing again, "You can repair your feet, you can repair your toes, but the owner of that slipper is in this oven."

So at that Mr. King walked around to the great big brick oven and poor Cinderella jumped out of the oven. The lady said, "Mr. King, don't look at that dirty girl."

Mr. King said, "I'll give her a chance." So at that Mr. King gave her some soap and water to clean her and as he presents the golden slipper to Cinderella she slipped it right onto her feet. Perfect fit. So she became the wife of the king.

We don't know in this case whether the storyteller actually broke into song when she recited Cinderella's singing from the dutch oven. If she did, the folklorist would classify this tale a *cante fable*. We know the following story to be such, as the raconteur sang the lines of the stuttering crewman to the tune of "Auld Lang Syne."

One time there was this boat and they had a crew of thirty-two, and one of them had a terrible time talking, stuttering everything he said. So one day he runs up to the captain and starts to speak, but all that came out was "Ahahahaha." And the captain says, "Oh, come on now, I haven't got time to hear you out, go tell it to the mate."

So he goes to the mate and the mate says, "Damn, man, don't bother me, tell it to Sweeney." And it goes on like that through the whole crew and nobody would listen to him. Well, during this time they were beginning to wonder why dinner was so late on board, and by and by this fella come running back to the captain. And just then the captain remembered that when this man sang he didn't stutter. In fact he was a good singer. So the captain says, "If you can't talk, sing." And he did:

> Should old acquaintance be forgot
> And never brought to mind,
> The colored cook fell overboard,
> About twenty miles behind.

Another older type of oral narrative, yet one that surfaces from time to time is the cumulative tale that builds on itself and draws the listener along. Here is Alex Kellam's rendition of a once widely told American yarn:

I heard this one about the rich plantation owner whose health went bad and the doctor ordered him away for six months' rest and he was to lose all contact with his friends and family. And so at the end of the six months he came back and his colored servant met him at the depot and took him home in the horse and buggy. On the way in he said to Sam,

"Now I've been gone six months and I haven't heard one thing from home. What's happened since I've been gone?"

He said, "Oh nothing, except one little thing. Since you've been gone your dog died."

He said, "The dog died? Well, what killed the dog?"

"Well, the dog eat some burnt horse flesh."

"Burnt horse flesh? How'd he get that?"

"Well, your barn burnt down and burnt up all the cows and horses, and after the fire the dog eat the burnt horse flesh and that's what killed the dog."

"Oh," he said, "my barn burned?"

He said, "Yessir, the barn burned."

He said, "How did the barn catch fire?"

"Well, it seems a spark flew over from the house and burned the barn down and burned up all the cows and horses and after the fire was over the dog eat the burnt horse flesh."

He said, "My house burned?"

He said, "Yessir, the house, that's completely destroyed."

"How did the house catch fire?"

"Well, it seems as though a candle caught to the curtain, the curtain caught to the roof, and fire, fire, and burned everything down."

He said, "They had candles burning in the house when we have gas and electric lights?"

"Yes, they had candles burning around the coffin."

"Coffin? Who's dead?"

"Oh yes, that's another thing I left out. It seems since you left your mother-in-law died."

"My mother-in-law died?"

"Yes, she's dead all right, you needn't worry about that."

"Well, what killed her?"

"Well, I don't know, but it seems it was from the shock of your wife a-running away with the chauffeur. But other than that there ain't no news."

Though it doesn't rely quite so much on formula, the tall tale derives its effect by drawing the audience along with the semblance of absolute truth, that is until the very end when the listener realizes that he has been completely duped. Many people believe that the tall tale is native to the United States, and in many ways its style and performance does fit the character of the nineteenth-century frontiersman and Mississippi raftsman well enough, but this type of story has roots in Europe. Tall tales seem to occur in two basic formats. In one context a group of wags sit around on the liar's bench trying to outdo one another with preposterous accounts. Such a session might begin with someone saying,

"Now around Easton, Pennsylvania, where I was one time, there was a place where you could holler and then take a cigarette out and light it before the echo got back."

"That's one hell of an echo, but it ain't nothing really. We were up to Alberta, Canada, north of Montana, and me and my partner parked our truck beside the edge of a canyon to go to sleep. And we wanted to be sure to wake up in the morning, so we went over and yelled in the canyon as loud as we could and then went back to the truck and went to sleep. Damned if seven and one-half hours later that echo didn't come back and wake us up."

Now the conversation turns to ships.

"You boys ain't never seen a ship. I was in Norfolk and one of these foreign boats came in for coal. And this one boat loaded ninety-five tons, every five minutes twenty-four hours a day for three weeks and never got her waterline underwater."

"Oh, that's nothing. I saw a ship once that it took one hundred and twenty-eight gallons of paint to paint a quarter of an inch bead line around her hull."

And so it might go on into the evening until one member of the cast uncorks a real whopper:

I was a small kid about ten years old and I have proof of this. We had a little shed out there where we used to have a cow and we closed it in and put some chickens in there. There was one white hen with some black feathers into her and my mother told me to go out there and see what she had laid. So I went out and I crawled in there and I brought in this egg that was as big as a goose egg and I gave it to her. The next morning my mother cooked that for breakfast and when she broke that on the frying pan it had six yolks in it. And that day I went out and got another egg and that one had five yolks in it and the next day four and then three and then two and one, and the next day when she broke that egg into the pan, it didn't have any yolk in it at all. And that's not all; listen to this: I know somebody who had a chicken that laid an egg with a perfect six double domino. Now if that weren't something!

With this perhaps the others concede and the gathering breaks up and they all head for home.

Along with this kind of tale swapping is the storytelling event where the narrator, with straight-faced demeanor and an ardent tone, spins a seemingly creditable account in order to put one over on his listener. Captain Al Wheatley caught me completely by surprise when he told me this story:

You know Thomas Crockett I was telling you about? . . . Well, he used to go crabbing when crabbing increased, and he used to keep these crabs in his float . . . And he said he had a crab in his float which he put there when he first started crabbing in the spring. And in September, every time he went to his float to sort the hard crabs out from the peelers, that same crab would be there whacking at him with his claws like that. [Gestures with his arms swinging around as though they were the claws of the crab.]

Well, one day he was out there and this crab was a-whacking at him, and he had one of these little canoes that had after lockers in them to keep the ballast stone in the middle seat for a middle sail. And he took his crab net and he eased this crab right over into the canoe. He said, "Never mind you son-of-her, when I get done fishing this float I'll fish you."

When he got done he went after this crab. He had on a pair of

hog hide boots, and he got up on the locker—that crab down
there a-whacking at him. Well, when he jumped down there for
that crab, both feet went out from under him—and he weighed
200 pounds or more—and his shins went up against the middle
seat, skinned them both the whole way up. He just lay there and
grunted and groaned, and after a while he turned and raised up,
and there was that crab at the end of the well a-whacking at him.
He put him in his crab net and eased him overboard and he got
in his skiff to go ashore. That crab followed him ashore still a-
whacking at him, and he pulled his skiff up on the bank, that crab
come right up on the edge of the bank after him.

Sitting in Wheatley's small living room watching the earnest
look on the man's face as he unraveled this yarn, I was completely taken in, made a fool of for believing that a crab could
actually possess such a common human trait as perversity. At a
different level, of course, this tall tale gives us a humorous look
at just how the waterman views those elusive crustacea on
which so much of his own welfare depends. In tall tales other
creatures take on human frailties. The snake, for instance:

Now I've always heard that country moonshine was powerful
around here, but this tale will bear me out. It seems that Mrs.
Morison's uncle and her father went fishing one time and as always they carried their jug along. They came to this water
moccasin who was just about ready to swallow a frog. So Mrs.
Morison's father took a forked stick and clamped it down over
the snake's head and took it [the frog] away 'cause they
wanted to use it for bait.

Well, that snake looked so darn downhearted that they gave
him a drink of moonshine, and off he went. So they went on with
their fishing and about an hour later one of them felt a tug on his
leg. He looked down and there was that snake back with another
frog. All I can say is, that must have been awful good moonshine.

Or the mosquito:

There were these two fellas going through town and when it
got dark they started to look for a place to spend the night.
Pretty soon they found this house and went into the bedroom.

Well, it was a pretty warm night and the mosquitoes were terrific. These two fellas covered themselves over with covers
and after a while one of them looked out and he saw a lightning bug, and he'd never seen one of them before, so he says
to his partner, "Jim, it's no use—we might as well give up;
they're hunting us with lanterns now."

At times the spirit of a hunting dog could even return from the
grave to help out his old master:

There was this fella down here one time and he had a wonderful rabbit dog. Well, this dog died and he decided that he had
to do something to remember him by so he had him skinned
and made himself a pair of gloves out of that dog's hide. One
time he was out in the forest working, and he pulled his gloves
off and laid them on this stump and set down to eat his lunch.
All of a sudden this rabbit run out of the underbrush and those
gloves jumped off that stump and grabbed that rabbit and
choked him to death.

And of course no collection of tall tales is complete without a
rendition of the ubiquitous story of "The Magnificent Hunt." In
this version from Garrett County the raconteur gives the yarn
more validity by sticking himself in the lead role.

I've been hunting going on fifty years now, but none of my experiences can equal the shot I made with that old muzzle-
loader the very last time I shot it. I was out by myself and I
only had enough powder to load one shot.
    Well, I climbed out of the lowlands through the brush and
laurel to higher land which was supposed to be loaded with
game of all kinds. (God, what a time I had getting that six-foot
muzzle-loader through that underbrush.) But I didn't have too
long before I came to some game. I looked up and there was a
big buck with antlers like a white oak tree and staring me right in
the face. But the funny thing was, just at the same moment I
noticed a big old black bear looking at me from a berry patch and
a flock of turkeys squawking over my head, and I looked to my
left and there was a groundhog about the size of a spring pig
scrambling out of his hole.

32

Well, I thought there was more choice meat on the deer than anything else, so I ups and let him have it. That thundering gun blew up right in my face. The shot hit the deer, the stock struck the groundhog, the barrel blew off and killed the bear and the ramrod caught those turkeys around the legs and held them tight.

Just about that time, I saw some honey running out of a hole in a tree—I've never been one to let anything go to waste—so I went to get a handful of leaves to stop the honey, and when I did I caught a rabbit by the ears.

Well, I loaded the game on my back and started for home, which was about four miles away. I didn't think I'd have too much trouble, but that oak tree that I was dragging behind me got rather heavy just as I reached the creek one-quarter of a mile from home. But anyway, I jumped into the creek with my hip boot flaps up, and that tree tied to my waist. The current got hold of me and just took me downstream. But I didn't get too mad, 'cause when I got out on the other side, I put my hand in my boots and I found I had about a bushel of bass in there, from about one to two feet.

So I got up on the bank and started for home. Now, I don't know if it was the weight of the nine turkeys in my pants' pockets or the rotten old thread that my Ma sewed my suspenders buttons on with, but while I was walking through the meadow to the house one of those buttons flew off and killed a pheasant flying overhead.

In some ways the tall tale has a modern analogue in the shaggy dog story. This kind of narrative also draws the listener along, but at the end instead of a laugh there is more often a long groan, as if to say, "My God, how could I have been stupid enough to waste my time listening to that." Many of these stories turn on belabored puns or the perversion of a proverb or advertisement. For example, there is this one, which must make the people in the telephone business wince:

Long ago in merry old England there was a king who wasn't too merry. His castle was being besieged by a bunch of barbarians. He knew the people could not ward off the attack themselves. He thought, "If only I could get help from a neighboring king." The kings in those days would help each other

33

out like that. So the king sent out one of his knights to take a message to another king. The only problem was that the knight had to cross a bridge that was guarded by two yellow hands. These hands would grab anyone who would try to cross the bridge.

So the knight went out, but never made it across the bridge. The king then sent out two more knights, but the yellow hands got them too. Then one of the king's page boys came up and pleaded to go. But the king said, "No." After the page boy pleaded and pleaded, the king finally relented because he was desperate. They just had to have help. When the page came to the bridge, he walked right across. The yellow fingers tried to get him but he was too small.

And the moral of the story is: "Let your pages do the walking through the yellow fingers."

2. Legends

PLACES AND EVENTS

ASIDE FROM the joke, the most common form of story told in Maryland is the legend. The legend differs from the märchen in that it is set in real time. The most common opening formula for the märchen, "Once upon a time . . . ," immediately sets the tale beyond the time frame of the everyday here and now. But when you hear a story that begins "When I was a child in Harford County, everybody knew about the ghost of Pedlar's Run," you have a time fix that anyone can readily identify with. What is more, you have real people and real places cited which lends a certain credibility to the account. That is one of the main points of the legend: It is told to be believed whereas the märchen, which exists in a world of seven-league boots and fairy godmothers, is told primarily for entertainment. Richard M. Dorson speaks about the legend this way:

Legends deal with persons, places, and events. Because they purport to be historical and factual, they must be associated in the mind of the community with some well known individual, geographical landmark, or particular episode. Any or all members of a given group will have heard of the tradition and can recall it in a brief or elaborate form. This indeed is one of the main tests of the legend, that it be known to a number of people united by their area of residence or occupation or nationality or faith. (Coffin, 155)

What occurs in the process of legend transmission is that a folk motif that has been floating about in oral circulation becomes attached to an applicable place or person and soon a story develops. In the case of supernatural occurrences that story often becomes the folk's way of explaining something that has,

35

for them, no scientific underpinnings—a strange light, an odd noise, an apparition. A bloodstain that cannot be removed invariably gives the folk the fodder for a legendary account, as in this tale from St. Mary's County:

> Down around here there's an old plantation called Mulberry Field. The owner of this place came home one time and found another man in bed with his wife. A fight started between the two men and the plantation owner killed the lover. They took him off to jail but because of the circumstances of the crime, he only got a two-year sentence.
>
> After the owner had served his sentence he came back to his plantation. He found a bloodstain on the floor, right where he killed that man. He tried to clean it up, but he couldn't get it off. So he had them come in and take the floorboards up and put new ones down. Those new boards were only in there one night and that stain appeared on them too. So then this man tried to cover up the stain with a rug, but the stain came right through the rug.
>
> They say he left that place and never came back, and that those stains are right there today.

In other examples of this motif an Eastern Shore waterman is struck and killed aboard his boat and the deck can never be scrubbed clean of his blood. In the attic of a Potomac, Maryland, home deep red stains on the floor commemorate the brutal slaying of a slave. In an Allegany County version, a Union soldier is robbed and murdered at an inn while returning home from the war. In his attempt to escape he lays a bloody handprint on the door and no one has ever been able to remove the stain. Around Thurmont the blood is actually on a gravestone, and I have seen photographs of a rust-colored blotch on the granite slab that attest to what the folk believe was a live burial:

> There's a tombstone around here that is said to bleed at certain times of the year. There was this man who was in a terrible accident. He was taken for dead and buried. They say around here— I didn't know him or his folks; I had friends that did—that he wasn't really dead when they buried him and that's why the stone bleeds. They say he tried to scratch his way out of the casket and that he broke his fingernails and wore his fingers down to the

bone and bled to death finally. They say that stone bleeds on the day he died. I don't know, but they say there're dark stains on that stone all the time.

Old houses anchor a number of legends that may start as part of a family tradition, but with time become absorbed in the folklore of the community. In Rawlings, a young woman named Rose lived with her family in one of the old houses there. She fell in love with a sailor who promised to marry her in June 1909, but on May 20th he ran off with another woman and Rose hanged herself in the front bedroom. Local residents vow that on full moon nights, if you know where to go to look, you can see her spectral form swinging from the rafters. A home in Midland afforded a much more gruesome tale. On Paradise Street there, a young husband took a butcher knife and killed his wife and children before he turned it on himself. As late as 1950, people in the area swore that a figure appeared night after night in the doorway of the room where the murders took place. The figure always carried a knife and his features seemed demonically possessed. Inexplicable screams also issued from the residence and startled nearby neighbors.

From Frederick came this strange account of a pair of shoes:

There is a huge old house in Frederick which at one time many years ago was the most beautiful estate in the county. It is old now and condemned and it's been vacant for thirty years. Yet no one will tear it down. It is said that the old woman who lived in the house was a very old person. She loved the old home so much that she would never leave it. She lived there with her daughter for many years. One night the old woman had a heart attack, but before she would let her daughter take her to the hospital, she wanted to put on her brand-new pair of shoes. So the daughter put the new shoes on her and placed the worn-out shoes on the hearth of the fireplace in the living room. The old woman died that night.

After the funeral, the daughter went back to the house to clear it out so that they could sell it. She saw her mother's shoes setting by the fireplace and tried to pick them up but they were stuck. A lot of people have tried to pull those shoes off but no one has ever been able to budge them. To this day those old shoes are still stuck on the hearth of that fireplace. People say that each night they see a figure walking into that house, yet all the doors and windows are boarded up. They see a light go on in the living room but there is no electricity in the house at all. Everyone says it's the old woman as she said she'd never leave that house. I've heard this story over and over from many people who believe it.

Urban dwellings at times provide spectral visitations as this story from Baltimore reveals:

Oh yes, there's another thing I know about the Hampton House. There was this young woman who lived out of town and she was invited to visit the Hampton House and she was passing through Baltimore one time and she decided to visit the family. When she drove up to the house she noticed it was very quiet, like no one was at home. Still, she went up to the door and knocked.

She stood there a long time, and just about when she was going to leave, the door opened and she saw an old Negro butler facing her. She thought it was strange that she hadn't heard him open the door. She told him that she'd come to see Mrs. Ridgely. He said that they were all on vacation, but he offered to show her around. Well he did; he took her all over that house and told her a lot of stories about it and everything. He said he knew so much about the house 'cause he'd been with the family for a long time. So when it was all done, the woman offered him some money, but he refused 'cause he said he had all he needed.

So on her way back through Baltimore again, she decided to call Mrs. Ridgely and tell her she'd been shown the house by this really well-informed butler. But when she talked to her on the phone, Mrs. Ridgely said she didn't have a butler, and when the woman described the man, Mrs. Ridgely said, "Why, my Lord, that's the old family butler. He died when I was a girl, and that's been thirty years or more now."

Landmarks other than old homes frequently furnish the necessary ingredients for legends. Isolated swamps, side roads, overgrown cemeteries, or wayside bridges provide just the right setting for mysterious lights or what appears to be a headless apparition. One of the best known legends of this sort is the tale of "Big Liz," the headless ghost of Gum Briar swamp near Cambridge, Maryland.

According to several residents, Liz was the slave of a wealthy landowner in the area who chose to bury his money out in the swamp, and to insure its protection he dragged Liz along, cut off her head and buried her beside the treasure. Given the right circumstances, she appears in the swamp with her head beneath her arm to ward off intruders.

Though a good many people in Dorchester County know of Big Liz, it has been the teenage crowd that has done the most to keep the legend alive. As is their style, they have devised a ritual which almost guarantees the appearance of Big Liz. On a dark night they drive to DeCoursey Bridge, park their car, blink the headlights three times and beep the horn six times. On schedule, Big Liz, with her head beneath her arm, emerges from the swamp and approaches their vehicle. Then, according to those who have been through the experience, as the specter closes on the car, the driver tries the ignition, but nothing happens. At the last moment, the engine coughs into life, and the car hurtles down the road, its occupants thoroughly chastened.

Bridge sites and headless ghosts often go together. On one of the bridges that crossed the C & O Canal near Cumberland, an Irishman was murdered and decapitated. For years men who operated the barges on the canal swore they saw the headless ghost of that Irishman, pipe in hand, sitting on the rail of the bridge as they passed beneath it. A similar instance in Harford County spawned a local legend:

> When I was a child in Harford County everybody knew about the ghost of Pedlar's Run. I was afraid to pass by there in an automobile; I'd hide my head to keep from looking.
>
> It seems that in the early days, a long time ago, pedlars would come through that county on foot carrying a pack with all their wares in it. They found this body by the run and it was buried under some rocks. But they couldn't find the head, so they buried the body without it.
>
> After that a lot of people reported seeing a headless figure

39

walking about in the area pushing a long stick into the ground. They said it was the pedlar's ghost looking for his head. I never saw him. Like I said, I was too afraid to look.

Not surprisingly, tales flourish about churches and cemeteries. For instance, unmistakable organ music issues from the darkened interior of a church on St. Andrews Road near the Hollywood Post Office in St. Mary's County, and people on occasion have seen strange lights flickering inside the sanctuary when no one is supposed to have been there. In the late sixties, an old boarded up black people's church on Colton's Point near Leonardtown reputedly held the ghost of the minister who would run off any white man who tried to enter. The preacher had apparently been murdered by white toughs years before, and white teenagers claimed his ghost had actually chased them from the premises when they tried to enter.

On the lower Eastern Shore where small family plots abound, the high water table demands shallow graves. Sometimes in severe weather these graves actually open up and in some cases cause bizarre incidents as this Venton woman describes:

When my aunt died, about a month after she died, her little daughter, Hilda, was out playing in this old woods here, and there come up a thunderstorm. She was staying with her grandmother at that time, and her grandmother went out and hollered to her to come in out of the storm. She had to holler twice for her.

When Hilda come, she was so tickled she didn't know what to do and she said, "Grandma, I seen Mom out there and she said when she goes back she's going to take me with her."

Now this sounds funny, I know, but inside of a month that kid died. What it must have been that kid really did see her mother out there in back where she was buried, 'cause after that storm they went out there and that grave was half uncovered; it was right wide open. It's the truth, I know, 'cause Pap and Ella and Meg, they went down there and filled it in. May have been lightning struck it, but I know that child seen her mother.

The author spent many hours gathering anecdotes, history, and other material from Maryland residents. He is shown here with Capt. Alex Kellam in 1968. (Photograph by A. Aubrey Bodine)

If places give rise to stories that linger in the folk memory, so do place names yield accounts that furnish etymologies that make sense in local communities. More often than not place name legends turn more on folk whimsy than on actual fact, but they have to be considered in the naming process since they may be the only rationale the local population has for a particular name. Rockawalking on the Eastern Shore, for instance, derives from an Indian term which loosely translated means, "the place where the creek comes in." Few if any local residents know that and when asked where the village got its name will tell you something akin to this:

> One time around here there used to be an old man called Rock. He didn't do very much walking. Everywhere he went, he either rode a bicycle or drove a horse and buggy. One hot day there was a group sitting under a shade tree at the end of a long lane. One gentleman looked up and said, "Look, here come Rock a-walking." From then on that's what this place has been called.

Similarly in the folk version, Accident, Maryland, got its name, not from a surveyor's mistake, but because an Indian borrowed a settler's axe. When he brought it back badly chipped, he said, "Axe, he dent."

At the end of one of those long peninsulas of land that drop away into the Chesapeake west of Princess Anne is a place called Deal Island. It wasn't always called that; it used to be called Devil's Island, just as a place a few miles up the road, Dames Quarter, used to be called Damned Quarter, according to eighteenth-century charts. These early names tally since we know two hundred years ago the English used certain parts of the remote Eastern Shore as a place to isolate their convicts and other ne'er-do-wells. In time, maps and charts began to carry Devil's Island as "Deil's Island," deil being an old English spelling for devil. By and by Deil's became Deal's and then Deal's became Deal. When I asked one of the local inhabitants what caused the final change, she explained: "They used to have an old wooden stamp in the post office, and the apostrophe 's' fell off."

Place name accounts can vary as does all folklore. Here for instance are two reasons for the name Silver Spring:

> Whoever was the owner of the Lee property had a daughter, and they were out riding one day. His daughter was apparently a very good horsewoman and she went on ahead of her father on her horse and as she was riding, the horse's hoof fell into a hole and threw her. When her father came up they discovered that the horse had fallen into a spring and when they saw it it reminded them of silver. There was just one spring so they called it Silver Spring—not Springs like in Florida.
>
> Silver Spring got its name from the mica spring under the big acorn. It was a very hot summer day and Montgomery Blair had dismounted from his horse. Then the horse ran away. When Blair found him he was drinking at this spring which was silvery from the mica. So Blair called it Silver Spring.

At times, a remarkable event will occur and that will take root in a family's storytelling tradition and become a part of their own cycle of family legends. The story will be brought up and recounted when family tales are told. In 1868, a Crisfield woman told me a story that had been passed down in her family for two generations.

Her grandfather, she explained, was a seafaring man of some renown. He owned and captained a number of vessels and spent a good part of his life freighting cargoes up and down Chesapeake Bay. One winter his son and another man were out in a small boat when a vicious storm came up and capsized the boat. Both occupants drowned. The companion's body was recovered the next day when it drifted ashore near Crisfield, but week after week slid by without any sign of Captain B's son. One night the father dreamed that his boy's corpse had drifted well up into a creek south of town. Next day with the place firmly etched in his mind, Captain B struck out across the marsh, and crawling on his hands and knees parting the marsh grass before him, came upon the bloated corpse of his son exactly where he'd dreamed it had been.

Odder still, perhaps, was the family legend of Captain B's experience aboard his own vessel. Bound up the Bay one sum-

mer morning, he looked forward from his position at the helm
and on top of the cabin house he saw what he thought for sure
was the perfect replica of a death's head. Forward of that he
noticed what seemed like the bodies of dead and dying people
spread liberally about the deck. No one else aboard saw a
thing. Captain B knew something out of the ordinary lay
ahead, and he seemed to know where, for he altered course and
within a short time they came upon an excursion boat engulfed
in flames. Around the burning hulk the water was full of
people, some swimming, others dead. Captain B and his crew
pulled as many people as they could out of the Bay and as their
boat turned away from the wreck and headed for Baltimore,
the captain now looked across his deck to see the exact picture
he had seen earlier that morning in his mind's eye—his deck
covered with bodies.

Strange encounters with fortune-tellers often become part
of a family's legend cycle. A Catonsville woman went down to
a particular seer who carried out her business on the District
line in Washington. She gazed into her crystal ball and saw
nothing at all. "Preposterous," cried the client, "look again."
She did, but still no image appeared. Furious, the patron
stormed out the door and was struck and killed instantly by a
passing automobile. A Baltimore fortune-teller was able to
clear up for a Crisfield woman an inexplicable event that had
happened thirty years before.

> Now Mrs. Wallace, who used to live out this way—her hus-
> band followed the water—and one time while he was away
> she was staying with her mother. And the family used to have
> an old slave named Jake. He lived with them through the
> years and his job was to keep the fireplace wood supplied and
> do all the handy work around the house. And on this particular
> night Mrs. Wallace and her mother were quilting and Jake
> brought in the wood and Mrs. Wallace said to him, "Jake,
> close the door." And he closed the door and sat down by the
> fireplace. Shortly after that the door opened again and Mrs.
> Wallace told him, "Jake, close that door."
> He said, "I did, ma'm."
> She said, "Well, close it." And he closed it and just as he sat

down, it opened again. And so Mrs. Wallace got up herself and went and closed it and latched it and it opened a third time, and it wasn't long after that she learned her husband had been drowned.

Now it was about thirty years after that that Mrs. Wallace went to visit her uncle in Annapolis with Mrs. Sterling and Mrs. Mc-Cready. And one day after dinner they decided to go up to Baltimore to have their fortunes told. Now Mrs. McCready was very well known to this spiritualist. Her name was Miss Childs. She had been an organist in one of those Baltimore churches but on this one particular night that she was to play, she couldn't turn a tune. She went absolutely blank and she said she was damned and she never played anymore. But she was able to read the future. And so these ladies went up to see her.

Now Mrs. Wallace said, "I'm going to be the first to have my fortune told 'cause I'm not going to allow you to go in there and tell her a lot of stuff about me and then have her tell it right back to me." So in the afternoon they went to Miss Childs's and when they were sitting in an adjoining room she came out and spoke to them.

She said, "I'm going to speak to this lady first." That was Mrs. Wallace. And she went in with Miss Childs and she said, "I ought not ever to talk with you. Today at noon you made fun of me and ridiculed me seriously, and I resent that. But since you've come all the way over here I will talk with you." And she took Mrs. Wallace's hand and she looked at it a minute or two and she said, "I see water everywhere and I see a man coming up and going down three times and I see a door opening and it opens three times."

Mrs. Wallace said, "Miss Childs, don't tell me anything more; I don't want to hear it." And she went out into the reception room.

THE DEVIL

The devil never acquired quite the reputation in Maryland he did in New England. The stern puritan conscience that seems to have tormented many of those early settlers imagined the evil one to be abroad on the landscape. Caves where the devil met

45

his minions still bear his name throughout New England and so do any of a number of rocks where he supposedly left the print of his cloven hoof.

In Maryland the devil does not appear as much in the names on the land as he does in stories of people who contracted with him for certain powers. It was simply the Faust legend set in the Old Line State. Best known in the Crisfield region was a man named Skidmore.

> Now Skidmore, he went out to a special place for nine consecutive nights and he waited and waited and on the last night the devil came to him. He wasn't frightened. And so the devil talked to him and gave him the power to do whatever he wanted to do, but none of it was motivated by a good spirit, just an evil spirit. From then on, if Skidmore wanted women, he could have women galore; if he wanted money, he could have all he wanted. That was why he was such a mystery.

When he received these special powers Skidmore put them to work in any of a number of ways. Once, two watermen were returning to Crisfield in their boat when they saw Skidmore floating around in Tangier Sound in a tub. The sight struck them as hilarious and they laughed till their sides ached. But Skidmore was not amused. He placed a curse on them, told them that this incident would come to their minds often, but before they could run to tell someone about it, the memory would slip away. And that is exactly what happened: One of the men would be out in his garden or up in the bow of a boat when the image of Skidmore in the tub would come to mind, but before he could get back into the house or into the stern of his vessel to tell the tale, there was nothing to tell. Not until Skidmore was dead did this story actually become known.

Storytellers on the lower Eastern Shore knew Skidmore better as a possessed worker than a magician. So widely did his reputation as a demon laborer flourish that it gave rise to a proverbial expression, and "to work like Skidmore" meant you were putting in a good deal more than a day's work. But it was evident that in Skidmore's case, his industriousness had infernal connections.

They used to say around here that you'd be going in the woods early in the morning where he'd been working and you'd hear more than a dozen axes going, hard as they could. And when you got up to him, you didn't see a soul but Skidmore around and he'd be sitting on a stump. But if you looked around you'd see any number of cords of wood, more than one hundred cords cut that very morning. But as soon as you'd leave you'd hear all those axes going again.

No one seemed to know whether the devil came to collect Skidmore's soul when he died as was the inevitable part of any contract of that sort. But, according to a Crisfield storyteller, there was no doubt about a man named Travis who lived over on Tangier Island in Virginia. He was a man of little means, living almost hand to mouth with his family on the island. Late one night while he sat by the fire smoking his pipe, a knock came on the door and a strange man told him that if he wished to change his style of living, to meet him at Job's Cove the next night. Travis went, and there he came face to face with the devil who told him to bury two brown pennies. When he did, the devil informed him that he had just sold his soul, and from that point on Travis prospered beyond his wildest dreams. But when he finally lay on his deathbed, this strange man appeared at the house, walked into the bedroom, and physically carried Travis away. All the relatives who had come to mourn the old man knew that he'd been in league with the devil all those years.

In the western part of Maryland a similar incident occurred:

Now this happened when we were living on Welsh Hill in Frostburg. Not far from us lived a mighty fine little woman. She was a good mother, a God-fearing woman, but she was married to an awful man, just a scoundrel of a man. He was just wicked and there was no hope for him. You know, he was just laying 'round all the time getting drunker and meaner—that was all. Well, one night our John come running in and said old Jack was stiff drunk. He was worse than he'd ever been before. Well, I says to your father, "We can't be leaving that little woman alone with that brute of a Jack in his condition."

47

So it was over to Mrs. Dautherty's I went to get her to come along with me. And we got a lantern, we did, and we went right over there. Now comes the startling part of what happened, and it really did happen, for Mrs. Dautherty saw it with her own eyes. We had just reached the bottom step of the porch, we had, when this thing passed us. It come like a big cloud of dust, right up out of the ground, that it did. And then something really hot brushed by us. We could both feel the heat. I couldn't be after describing it. We could only tell it had hooves, but they never touched the ground.

Me and Mrs. Dautherty was so frightened at first that neither one of us could be after speaking. We just gripped each other by the hand and made the sign of the cross, 'cause we knew we were in the presence of something evil. After a bit I was able to speak again, I said, "Sure enough old Jack is gone. I've always been hearing he sold his soul to the devil."

And to be sure, when we got into the house old Jack was dead.

George Bender of Hebron also worked up a contract of some sort with the devil. He used to play the horses. Not long after he linked up with Old Scratch, he began to win a great deal of money, but people noticed that while he stood watching the races, two tall black men always came and stood beside him. When they did, his horse immediately began to pull away from the field.

Everything went along fine for Bender for quite some time; financially he was all set. One summer afternoon a waterman friend of his was bound down the Bay aboard his boat. All at once he was shaken out of his reverie by what he thought was the apparition of George Bender at the reins of two black horses surging across the waters of the Bay. "Aren't you George Bender?" the waterman cried after him.

"Yes, I am George Bender," he replied, "and I'm on my way to hell." Sure enough, when the waterman returned home to Hebron, he discovered that Bender had died that same day.

A Dorchester County man relinquished his soul to the devil for gold. According to the deal, he was to hang a boot beneath the chimney and the devil would fill it with coins each morning. But his greed got the best of him, and he cut a hole in the foot of the boot, and the living room filled up instead. The devil discovered the ruse soon enough and carried off the man's soul to hell long before the appointed time.

Not many outwitted the devil, but Molly Horn was one. She and the devil contracted to farm on the Eastern Shore together. They agreed that on the first crop Molly would take what grew in the ground and the devil would take what grew on top. Molly planted white potatoes and the devil came out shortchanged. So for the next crop they decided to do it the other way round, the devil getting what grew in the ground. This time Molly planted peas and beans and once more the devil got nothing. A hot argument ensued on the bank of the North West Fork of the Nanticoke River in Dorchester County. Molly struck the devil a terrific crack and skidded him across the marsh to the edge of the Bay. When he stood up and shook the mud off himself, it formed Devil's Island, then he dove overboard and made Devil's Hole.

If the devil appeared to collect defaulted souls, it was also commonly assumed that he showed up at card games when money changed hands, at least so claimed a Hancock raconteur:

> One night my grandpap and grandmam went to a square dance in Hancock. After a time they got tired of dancing and sat down to rest for a while. Grandpap heard that there were several games of cards going on in the next room and so he decided that he'd like to join in. My grandmam was very much against playing cards, but anyways he went in there in spite of her warning.
>
> When he got into the room he saw several of his friends and one stranger at the table. These fellas said, "Come on over, Julian, we need another player." So grandpap sat down and started to play. No one introduced him to the stranger, and as it later turned out, no one had ever seen him before. But pretty soon, they found out that the stranger was quite a card player and he kept winning and winning.
>
> At one point grandpap dropped one of his cards on the floor and when he stooped down to pick it up, he noticed that the leg on the stranger looked like a horse's leg, had a hoof on it, and he

49

had a tail. And when he looked up, there was no one in that chair. The stranger had vanished. One of the men at the table said he'd gone right through the floor. And there are a couple of other men who were right there that night who are still living and they swear that is a true tale.

WITCHCRAFT

Witchcraft has figured in Maryland folklore as it has elsewhere for a long time. Though witchcraft in Maryland never gained the notoriety it did in New England, we have proof that the witch has been abroad in the Free State since the seventeenth century. To be sure, her antics as portrayed in the tales of more recent storytellers lack some of the luster and command less fear than did the witches of two centuries ago. Yet then as now, it seems a witch was invariably shaped by her environment and the attitudes of the community where she lived.

Take a hypothetical instance. A woman, let us say, is slightly eccentric. In the city, there's nothing alarming about being eccentric, but in a small rural community someone who is odd, or who has a deformity of some sort—a withered limb, a shrunken countenance—becomes marked by the local folk. Ostracism pushes her to the edge of the community where she lives alone, sometimes with a collection of cats. In time her physical appearance deteriorates. She dispenses simples and herbs. Most important, her isolation gives her the opportunity to observe at close hand the comings and goings of people in the community, so much so that some of her predictions become prophetic, or so it seems to the villagers. They credit her with occult powers, and her identity is established: She is a witch. From that point on, the legendary process begins. Every unaccountable illness, every freak storm, every crop failure gets billed to her account and her place in the community's folk tradition is secure.

Such was the case with Moll Dyer whose death and subsequent curse have spun their way through the repertoires of St. Mary's County storytellers for several centuries. Dyer came to this country in the 1700s. Even after she lived in St. Mary's

County for a while no one knew much about her. There were those who claimed she came of high birth, but left the old country to escape a mysterious event in her life she could not deal with. Once settled outside Leonardtown, she lived very much to herself in a remote cottage, and her reputation as a witch began to take hold when she was seen out gathering herbs and simples. Soon tales began to be told about the spells she was able to cast on animals and people alike, and it wasn't long before any misfortune in the region was set on her head. Finally when an epidemic swept through the county, the residents had had enough. One winter night they gathered themselves some torches and set fire to Moll Dyer's cottage hoping to catch her inside. But the poor woman learned beforehand of their intentions and fled into the woods. There she knelt on a stone and issued a curse upon the land and her persecutors. Several days later a child found Moll frozen to death on the rock, still in that supplicant position.

To this day the rock where Moll reportedly knelt still shows the imprint of her knees. And the curse she issued in her final prayer came to pass. The land where her cabin stood has always been a barren place, never producing any crops, and according to local accounts, several of the descendants of those who once torched Moll's house were actually consumed when their own houses burned to the ground. Early tradition held that Moll made frequent appearances on the anniversary of her death, and had been seen dashing across some deserted back roads as if pursued. A Drayden woman living in the 1960s recalled her father's tales of a headless horseman (presumably one of Moll's tormentors) who appeared occasionally near the stone.

Not all Maryland witches generated such a cycle of tales as Moll Dyer. More typical perhaps would be Aunt Hanna who lived in Crisfield. Harold Hinman remembered her:

> Old Aunt Hanna, oh yes, she was considered a witch by the local people around here. Now I remember her and I know right when this happened. She used to work for my mother back then, and one day she got mad with Mom and she threatened to put a spell on her. When Mom was cleaning up

trash, Hanna put a bottle of pins in that trash. So my mother
put that trash in the fire along with the pins and the bottle ex-
ploded and the pins stuck into her. Just one of Hanna's tricks,
you know.

Samantha Rayfield also had a story.

Now my mother used to tell me about Aunt Hanna; she used
to live around here and she was supposed to be a witch.
That's what they said anyway. Well, one day some people
were going by the door of her house and she was sitting right
there in the doorway spinning at her spinning wheel. So a little
while later they come back that way and Aunt Hanna was out
in back of her house picking tomatoes, but that wheel was
a-spinning away all on its own. And a bit after that, some
friends of my mother's passed by her house, and they saw her
out tending her chickens, but that spinning wheel was working
away, all by itself. Now that was really something, I guess.

In nearby Mount Vernon on the lower Eastern Shore, the local
witch was a black woman named Henny Furr. She conjured
harassment in a variety of ways. When a neighbor's coon dogs
wandered into her yard, she bewitched them so that they
turned on their master and drove him off his own property. At
another time, Henny helped John Cullen who was squabbling
with Ely Taylor over property rights. Henny brewed up a po-
tion which she slipped into Taylor's coffee one morning, but his
daughter drank it instead. For three days she passed nothing
but snakes. Taylor was understandably upset and sent for the
doctor, but his medicine brought no cure. Next he turned to
another local conjure woman in the town. She placed a pound
of tenpenny nails in an envelope, threw it on a platter, poured a
pint of whiskey over it and lit it on fire. When the flames sub-
sided, the platter reflected the remarkable likenesses of John
Cullen and Henny Furr. "Now," the conjure told her client,
"take this whiskey bottle and bury it in Henny's yard." Taylor
did and his daughter improved at once.

Sometime later Henny was caught ravaging a cabbage
patch after dark. A farmer complained that something had
been ruining his crop for quite a while. Finally one evening he

took his gun and when he saw a strange animal darting through the planted furrows, he drew and fired. Next day he learned that Henny Furr lay in bed at home, riddled with shotgun pellets.

Similar tales surrounded a Hopewell woman long suspected of witchcraft. She developed a strong dislike for a particular waterman. One day when the unlucky fellow was out working the water on his boat, she etched his picture, then took it down and placed it at the water's edge. When the tide came up and covered her artwork, the man fell overboard and drowned. On another occasion, she drew a picture of someone who displeased her and hung it on the wall. Then she loaded a shotgun with pieces of a dime that she had cut up, drew a bead, and fired at the picture. The man fell dead in the Hopewell railroad station.

Usually though, it was the witch herself who succumbed to a load of silver buckshot:

Now this woman I'm going to tell you about lived down in Hunting Creek on the Eastern Shore of Virginia. My grandmother said this was a true story. There was this waterman and his name was Jim Canon and one day he was tying up at the wharf and this woman who they said was a witch came down there just as he come in. Well, he had two baskets of hard "jimmie" crabs and a basket of fish. She came up to him and she wanted that mess of fish. He said, "Lady, to tell the truth, I just got enough for myself, but I got some hard crabs. Do you want them?" They were good lively ones, too.

Well, she put her hand down in that mess of crabs and they all dropped their claws and everyone of them died. She put a spell on those crabs. So he got mad when he saw he'd lost all that money and he started for home and she said, "You'll be sorry for this. Won't give me that mess of fish."

That night he went down to the local store and on his way home she overtook him and turned him into a beast of burden of some sort, a horse or mule or something, and she rode him all the way to Cape Charles, some hundred miles through marsh and brambles and bushes, just to get some wish he'd refused her. So when he come home he was all cut up with briars and everything and all out of breath so that his wife called a doctor.

53

The next day he got a gun shell and he took out all the buck-shot and he put in some pieces of silver and he wadded it back in and he drawed a picture of that old woman as best he could and he put that on the wall and shot at it. And a day or so after that she got sick and died, and they say where the silver hit that picture is where it hit her—in the legs, breast, and stomach.

There were a number of ways to break witch spells or ward off evil. A broom across the door or a little salt sprinkled around the house kept the home hex-free. Some people went so far as to pound nails into boards. Then they slept with the boards on their chests, points up, to keep witches from riding them at night. A Frostburg woman remembered an effective way of keeping witches away from the horses:

> Quite a number of years ago around here, the Standard family started to have some real trouble with their horses. Every morning when they should have been rested after a good night, those horses were tired and wet with perspiration. No one had any idea how to solve the mystery, but someone said what it might be was ghosts or witches riding the horses at night.
>
> Well, one day this old tramp came to the Standard's place. He was after some food and when they gave it to him they started to tell him about their trouble with the horses. So this tramp was so grateful for the food that he said he'd help them out. That night he nailed a screen over all the windows and doors of the place where they kept the horses. He said a ghost or witch would have to go through every one of the holes in that screen before he could get in to bother those horses. And sure enough, after that, the Standards never had any more trouble with their horses being tired.

Another Frostburg woman had a confrontation with a local witch and that evening when she went home to churn her butter, she worked for hours without success. Finally she called a friend and explained the situation. Her friend took a poker, heated it up in the fire, then walked next door and plunged it into the woman's butter. The next time the woman encountered the witch, she noticed a bad burn scar on her hand and presumed it was from the poker.

Not all women who dabbled in the occult were necessarily malicious. If treated respectfully or paid well enough some could bring about a run of good luck or fair weather. It is a well-known fact that as late as the nineteenth century, mariners frequently sought the help of local witches to secure fair winds for a long sea passage. The good weather came in the form of a piece of line tied in three knots and the admonition: If you wish more wind, untie the first knot, more still, undo the second knot, but whatever you do, never undo the third knot. Those who failed to heed the warning, and lived to tell about it, spoke of a vicious storm striking the vessel as soon as they untied the third knot. Though we know of no women in Maryland who actually trafficked in wind and weather in the twentieth century, there was an old woman in Friendsville who magically shored up a sagging business and tried to add some luster to an otherwise lusterless face.

> There was this lady around here who owned a store. She'd had it quite a while and business just wasn't prospering too well. So she decided to go to this other wise old woman who everyone said could help you out if you had problems like this. No one knew how she did it, but she seemed to have some special sort of power. This lady who owned the store went in and asked this wise old woman how she could improve her business. This old woman told her to take a large white handkerchief and put an old mouse skin, four pebbles, and a bit of powder in it. Then she told her to take it and shake it three times at each corner of her store and her business would begin to get better.
>
> Well, that lady did what she was told, took that old handkerchief and shook it like that and, sure enough, business began to pick up right away.
>
> Another time there was this ugly girl who'd heard of this wise old lady and she thought if she went to see her, perhaps she could become pretty. So this wise old woman asked her if she ever used rouge. The girl said, yes, she did. This woman told her to take the rouge exactly one mile from her house and bury it.

Then she was to visit that spot where she'd put it each day until she could no longer find the rouge when she dug it up. Well, she did that, but I don't think it ever helped her looks too much.

TREASURE LEGENDS

A typical treasure legend might run something like this: For years in a small seaside village word has had it that Captain Kidd's treasure lies buried out on the marsh. Townsfolk have seen strange lights flickering there at night and one evening two young men decide to go see what's out there. They grab picks and shovels and head across the marsh and begin to dig. Three feet down, the pick strikes metal, and one of the diggers cries, "We've got it." Suddenly there is a piercing cry and the men look around to see a specter on a fire-breathing horse bearing down on them. They drop their tools and light out back across the marsh for home and some hard liquor. The next day they return to the site only to find their picks and shovels strewn randomly about, but no hole and no treasure.

Built into this composite account are the usual ingredients one often finds with such stories: The inexplicable lights (thought to be spirits guarding the treasure), the broken taboo when someone speaks before the treasure is above ground, the retaliation of the guardian spirit, and the ultimate disappearance of the treasure.

Not every treasure legend has all the parts, but the underlying reason for their existence stems from the human desire to get rich very quickly. It is this common motive that drives otherwise sensible men to do seemingly foolish things, though they may well rationalize their quests in newspaper reports such as this one from the nineteenth century which described a Massachusetts group that discovered

a cave with an entrance six to eight feet in height, and upwards to one hundred feet long, with two apartments. In the first they found some earthenware and a large stone cross ... A number of citizens, with a lantern, subsequently entered the second apartment where they found a skeleton seated on a huge iron chest, with its back resting on the wall. On opening the chest they found that it contained gold coin, perfectly smooth on one side, and a cross with some characters on it on the other. The gold in the chest by weight is worth seven hundred and fifty-three dollars. (Newburyport *Daily Evening Union*, Feb. 27, 1852)

If New England had Captain Kidd reportedly burying his treasure in any of a thousand coves and crannies along the coast, so did the Chesapeake Bay have Blackbeard (sometimes called Bluebeard) who set his loot ashore on islands and along rivers on both the eastern and western shores. Historical records claim that Blackbeard never ventured much beyond the capes at the entrance to the Bay, but storytellers have him going as far north as the Choptank River where he supposedly threw an oaken chest overboard. Not surprisingly, on Smith and Tangier islands in the middle of the Bay stories circulate about the pirate's legacy. A Rehobeth, Maryland, woman who grew up on Tangier Island remembered hearing this long story in the 1920s:

> My mother used to tell us this, told it to her grandchildren too, and she used to keep them spellbound with the story of Bluebeard. It went something like this:
>
> One time there was a very poor man and he had four children. Nothing he ever tried amounted to anything and the harder he worked, the less he seemed to have. So one night he was sitting around the local store over there on the island, and the men got to talking about pirates, mostly about this pirate Bluebeard and how he used to go around hijacking ships and taking the cargo for himself. They told how he got richer than anyone could imagine and just before he was captured, he took all that treasure and buried it. And they said his spirit was still wandering around the island trying to find someone to tell where the treasure was 'cause his spirit couldn't rest until he'd given away all his gold.
>
> Well, this fellow listened and he wished he could have some of that gold. On his way home he had to pass this old deserted house. But before he got there the wind started to whine and moan in the trees, and as he got near the house, he heard this voice whispering in his ear and it said, "Can I speak with you?" Well, this man was scared out of his wits and he started to run along the road, but he heard the voice very close by say again, "Please let me speak with you."

So this man stopped and stuttered and said, "What do you want with me?"

And the voice said, "I'm the spirit of Bluebeard the Pirate and I want you to have my money; I must give it to someone before I can rest, so if you will come to this old deserted house at midnight Saturday, I'll meet you here and you will never want for anything more as long as you live."

Now that old fella, he ran all the way home as fast as he could, but he never told a soul what he'd heard out there on the marsh, but all week he kept thinking about meeting that ghost out there by that deserted house. But he kept telling himself he just had to do it for his family.

He thought Saturday would never come, but when it did it was cloudy and cold and dismal. The family went to bed early and after everyone was asleep he crept out of bed and put on his clothes and buttoned up his raggedy old coat around his neck and pulled this old felt hat down over his eyes and started out for that place.

When he got there, he crouched down near an old tree and waited. All of a sudden the sky got dark and the wind began to howl and he felt this hot breath against the back of his neck. Well, he just couldn't take it; with the last bit of strength he had, he gave a screech and jumped to his feet and took off for home. And when he got there, he crawled into bed and never let anyone know what had happened that night.

So that ended that little episode. But one of the children in the family was a boy about twelve years old. He was sort of retarded and couldn't attend school, and he used to wander in the woods a lot, and almost everyday he would come home with all these gold pieces and throw them on the table and say, "Look at these shiny things, aren't they pretty."

And his father would say, "Where did you get this?"

And he'd say, "A dark man with a long blue beard gave it to me and he told me to come back and he'd always give me some more every time I returned."

And so that man knew it was really Bluebeard who was giving the boy the money he was too frightened to take away.

Farther up the Bay "a devil of a man" named Captain Francis

worked his piracy on a variety of vessels, and then hid out from his pursuers in the Rhode River below Annapolis. People in the area believed he buried his treasure in the cellar of an old house on some property there. A man from the Washington area bought the property and built himself a house a ways back up from the original structure. His foreman came to him one day and told him someone had been hard at it digging around in the cellar of the old house, and when he inspected it he found it all torn up. The owner never learned whether anything was discovered, but he was sure it was the strength of the legend about Captain Francis that brought the treasure seeker to his property.

Out in the western part of the state it is General Braddock who, according to local hearsay, buried his treasure in the countryside around Frostburg. No one knew exactly where. One man thought the general had put it under John's Rock since the rock, once a huge solid piece, had been split in half by treasure hunters. Another local wag maintained that the treasure had been put in an old shed along the Midlothian Road near Braddock Park. On what did he base this theory? Well, the man who owned the shed never had a penny until he finally tore the building down. Then he became suddenly prosperous, built himself a new house and a large barn, and never seemed to want for anything. But Ted Brode, another Frostburg resident, disagreed; according to his account the secret of the treasure still lay with the dead.

> You know General Braddock's trail which goes both east and west on what is now Hansel's farm in western Frostburg? Well, that's the hiding place of General Braddock's treasure. When we were kids we used to spend a lot of time hunting for that treasure. Everybody did, but nobody could ever find it.
>
> At the foot of Hansel's farm, down along George's Creek, was where one of the first coal mines was. Boys used to begin working in that mine when they were thirteen years old. We used a rope and wheel then; didn't have any cars. My uncle, Jim Brode, and another fella claimed they found Braddock's treasure. They were going to get it on the night after they discovered the hiding place. But they didn't tell anybody where it was 'cause they wanted it all for themselves. That day they went to work in the

coal mine and the mine caved in and killed both of them, and that's as close as anyone's ever come to finding that treasure.

Common folks as well as generals and pirates saw fit to hoard their money. At one time old Jess Winebrenner owned most of the land around Eckhart, Maryland, and everyone knew he had plenty of money. His children recalled that every so often at night, Jess would take a lantern and a spade and go out wandering on the land to bury some of his wealth. But they never dared follow him, since he swore he'd kill anyone who did. When Jess died, he took his secret with him. Still, the family began to look for the money in a cave on the property, but such odd things occurred while they were digging, that they gave up, figuring the old man had put a curse on the money and didn't want anyone else to have it.

In Cumberland tales circulate about a man named Grahams who at one time owned all the land from the bottom of Grant Street to Wrights Crossing on both sides of the road. Grahams had done exceedingly well and openly bragged to his friends that he buried his fortune on his property. As recently as 1948, on the anniversary of Grahams's death, a strange light appeared on what was once his property, then gradually moved to a particular spot where it burned itself out. Declared a Hoffman, Maryland, woman:

> This is as true as I'm sitting here, 'cause Helen, when she was only a little thing, she seen it. And my husband's seen it, too. He was scared stiff and came right home. Lots of others have seen it too, and they're dead sure it's right where the money is, but most people when they see it are too scared to do anything.

Grandma Hicks, according to her granddaughter, came from Wales and settled in Cumberland. During her life she was extremely thrifty and never believed in banks. When the old woman died, the granddaughter and another relative went into the cellar of the house where the old woman lived and began to dig. Everything went along fine until they got down about two feet and then long sheets of flame erupted out of the ground as high as their heads. It didn't take them long to forget about the money. They left a lot quicker than they came, reckoned

Screen painting, which began as an attempt to provide privacy in an urban environment, soon became a significant folk art. This East Baltimore resident sits in front of her painted screen door. (Photograph by Erick Hoopes, courtesy of the Painted Screen Society of Baltimore, Inc.)

Grandma Hicks's spirit didn't want them messing around in that cellar.

On the King Farm in Ellerslie, Maryland, the ghost of a black slave guards the family treasure. During the Civil War, the owner joined the Confederates and departed, leaving his estate in the care of the slave. When the Yankee soldiers came, the slave buried all the family money and valuables on the place, but he was killed before he could tell anyone where. The master returned after the war, looked everywhere but found nothing. As late as 1950, residents of the King Farm spoke of seeing the ghost of a black slave wandering the grounds, presumably still safeguarding the family treasure. Or was he really? Perhaps he wanted to tell someone brave enough to accost him where the treasure was. Sometimes a spirit can't rest until it has let its secret be known. Take the Cline family of Frostburg, for instance. They came by their good fortune this way.

> At one time the Clines used to live over there in Shovetown. You know where the old log house burned down right on the turn there in back of Byrne's store? Well, that's where they lived and in them days they didn't have nothing.
>
> Well, before the Clines moved into that house there used to be an old man, a bachelor, who lived there. People knowed he had money but when he died nobody ever found it. But when they moved in there, it wasn't very long before one day Mrs. Cline was in the kitchen all by herself and the ghost of that old man appeared before her just as plain as day. Well, this ghost was standing before the flue and he was rubbing his hands up and down the chimney saying all the time, "You're still in there and I can't rest. Nobody's found you and I can't rest."
>
> Mrs. Cline she got scared and she ran out of the house screaming, and she ran across the road to the next house. When she got there she told the neighbor woman—I forget her name— what she saw. So this woman told her the next time the ghost appeared in the house she should say, "In the name of God, what do you want?" And then the ghost would answer her.
>
> It wasn't long after that that Mrs. Cline saw that ghost come and do the same thing again, so she said what she'd been told, "In the name of God, what do you want?" And the ghost told her

she was to take the third row of bricks from the bottom of the chimney and she'd find the money the old man had put there. Then that ghost just disappeared.

Well, Mrs. Cline did what she was told and she found three or four gallon jars jam-packed with all kinds of money. I never heard how much they got, but it was a hell of a lot. Mrs. Cline gave her neighbor about half a jar for helping, and it wasn't long after that that the Clines moved into Frostburg, set themselves up in business, and bought a couple of houses. They did fine for a long time, but that's how they got their start, and that's the gospel truth.

3. Folk Heroes and Local Characters

IT WOULD BE a sorry folk community indeed that could not come up with at least one folk hero, local wit, eccentric, town fool, miser, or village indigent. People, like places, produce the fodder for legends, and the cycle of tales that develop around an individual gathers its momentum from a much larger source of floating tales and folk motifs that circulate in oral tradition. For example, this story got pinned on a derelict in Grahamtown:

> You know every town has its habitual drunkard, and Grahamtown was no exception. There it was Davey Dikes, and he was really the main character in the town, too. So this one Easter eve, Davey got all looped up. He went to town and on his way home he had to go through the cemetery there. There was this freshly dug grave there and as luck would have it, he fell down in it and couldn't get out.
>
> Come morning, Davey heard someone walking by and he started yelling for help. So this person walks over to the grave and looks down in there and called to see who it was. Davey yells back: "It's Davey Dikes, by God, the first man up on Resurrection Day."

What might fool the naive listener as a true story turns out to be a tale widely known in the area and elsewhere. In nearby Eckhart it's Boggy Eisentrout who falls in the grave after polishing off four gallons of beer, then on Easter morning peers over the lip of his resting place and shouts, "Great Jupiter, it's Resurrection Day and I'm the first one up." And across the border in Wellersburg, Pennsylvania, John T. utters the witty remark from a newly dug grave.

64

Though reduced in scale, the process that produces characters such as this is the same one that went into creating a legendary figure like Davy Crockett. We know Crockett made a reputation for himself as a hunter and crafty backwoodsman in Kentucky early in his life, but it wasn't until he was elected to Congress and went to Washington that his prowess gained national recognition, thanks to journalists who found him good copy. Many of his escapades were preserved in print, and after his death, as is often the case with heroes in folk tradition, the legend grew larger than the man and accounts about Crockett took on almost mythic proportions.

Seldom does a local figure get foisted on the national consciousness the way Crockett was, yet people in any given folk community will frequently extend a man or woman in tale or song well beyond the moment of his or her death. All a local person needs are those characteristics that the group admires or finds humorous, and his place in the local pantheon is pretty well secured.

In my collecting on the lower Eastern Shore of Maryland I ran across a number of these local heroes; probably the best known to the storytellers of Smith Island and Crisfield was William Bradshaw. But no one called him William. He was known simply as "Lickin' Bill," and this was not, as one might suppose, because he could lick any man on the shore, which he doubtless could, but because of a strange proclivity to lick things with his tongue. Aboard a dredge boat the urge would come on him to lick the masthead block, and the crew would have to lower the sails and let him climb to the top of the mast to satisfy his wish.

Apparently he was a huge man, as Alex Kellam recalled.

I remember Lickin' Bill. I was real small when he died, though. He had a goatee that used to come down to his waist; practically all the older men of the day wore mustaches. I'd say he was about six-eight or -ten, and he weighed two hundred and seventy-five pounds. Course, there was no tailoring in them days, and they said it was an awkward-looking thing to see him going to church with his pants legs just below his knees and his coat sleeves up to his elbows.

On his feet Lickin' wore size fourteen brogans which at times became frightening instruments. Three toughs down on the Eastern Shore of Virginia came on him once outside the local store. He cold-cocked the first boy with one blow, grabbed the second one, and threw him end over end twenty feet in the air. The third fellow turned and fled and as he went by Lickin' kicked at him and missed, but his shoe came off in the effort and struck the weatherboarding plank on the side of the store and split it clean through.

Bradshaw's brute power caught the imagination of the local island people. He came out of a time when things were done, as one man put it, "by main strength and ignorance." A character who could out-muscle any comer rose quite naturally to a position of respect. Lickin' Bill never lost a wrestling match on the island and there were those who came from quite far away to take him on. Island men used to play a game with Bradshaw to test his strength. They'd have him hold a broom handle at arm's length, then hang weights on it to make him release it, but the broom handle always broke first. Once, while slaughtering hogs, Lickin' swung the axe round with one hand but the axhead came off at the top of the arc. Still, just the force of the blow with the handle killed the creature instantly.

Lickin' Bill had two other qualities that appealed to the local folk. He was a very devout Methodist and he was "witty"; that is, he knew how to deliver the appropriate remark at the right moment. Many of those remarks came in church at the expense of the preacher.

> Well, there was this man over there on the island there and he had been a preacher and they said he was a right good one. So he got after the camp meeting committee to let him preach the opening sermon. He thought he deserved the honor, you know. So the committee got together and they said, "Well, boys, he's done a lot of good work, been a big help around here, he's a hard worker, let's let him preach the opening sermon."
>
> And so he picked his text and he got up and began. "And they casted forth seven anchors and waited for the break of day." Well, everything left him. He just went blank. So he walked backwards and forwards there a couple of times and he stopped and pointed down his finger and said, "And they casted forth seven

anchors and waited for the break of day." Still didn't come. It was a blank. So he made a couple more passes and he stopped and he pointed and he said, "And they casted forth seven anchors and waited for the break of day."

Old man Lickin' Bill jumped up and said, "Brother, that's twenty-one anchors, that'll hold any vessel in Tangier Sound."

George Davey of Fairmount also had the reputation of being an Eastern Shore strongman. One fellow, hearing of his reputation as a fighter, came over all the way from the western shore to challenge him. People at the local store told him Davey was down working on the waterfront. He went down to find him, but when he met Davey coming up from the water with a thirty-foot boat on his back, the would-be challenger turned around and left. On another occasion while delivering oysters to Baltimore, a vessel deliberately pulled in front of Davey's boat and wouldn't let him out. After some hot words, Davey walked forward, cradled the other boat's bowsprit in his arms, and broke it clean off at the knightheads. Then they departed. One man reported that Davey had once agreed to lug a neighbor's boat to the water for a five-dollar fee. He did the job, but when the neighbor balked at paying him, he hauled it right back up onto the shore. That same story is told on "Strong Ross" Henry of Salisbury who when refused payment for hauling someone's Model T out of a ditch, put it right back in.

Equally revered with the strongmen on the Eastern Shore were the saints. Best known, of course, was Joshua Thomas who in the early 1800s went around spreading the gospel to the island folk in his log canoe, *Methodist*. Much of his good work has been documented in Adam Wallace's 1861 study, *The Parson of the Islands*, but oral tales still linger among Eastern Shore storytellers which detail Thomas's Christ-like activities.

There was no questioning his power to heal the sick and lame. On two separate occasions Thomas needed transportation by boat. In both instances he asked watermen who had been invalided to take him. Both refused, blaming their infirmities, but when Thomas prayed that they be healed, they both turned up at dockside the following morning ready to take the parson to his destination. Thomas also used his special powers to bring sustenance to the needy:

Well, we were speaking about Joshua Thomas, what a good man he was. Well, we had another native on Deal Island that was a very sick man. He couldn't eat anything but fish and he just craved a piece of fish. And the doctor said to him, he said, "You can't get no fish now, because you haven't any way to catch them because you haven't got no crabs."

And this man named Joshua Thomas told the brother of the sick man to go down under a stump on Little Island and he would look in the hollow of a root at a certain place there and he would find one crab, and he would take that and go down to the south end of Little Deal Island and he would throw his line out, and he said he would get one bite and that would be a rockfish.

Well, that fellow did that and sure enough, it was just like Joshua Thomas said. He went there and got that crab and caught that rockfish and brought it back to his brother.

When Thomas appears in the stories of most good Methodists on the Eastern Shore, it is invariably to record some miraculous activity, but in at least one tale the parson suffered the fate of many preachers in that region and became the butt of humor.

Now I was told this by Mrs. Anderson who used to run the boardinghouse on Deal Island. She said Joshua Thomas had these false teeth, and he lost them overboard one time. Everyone came around to help to see if they could find them. One young boy dove over to see if he could find them. Some of the men there used their tongs to see if they could get the teeth that way. Nobody had any luck.

Finally there was this woman that came along. She said she'd get them. So she went home and pretty soon she came back with this thing in her apron which had a long piece of string tied to it. She threw that overboard and it wasn't long before she brought up those teeth. They all asked her how she'd done it.

She said, "There's only one way to catch a Methodist's teeth: With a piece of fried chicken."

A Somerset County man once remarked to me, "We are one of the poorest counties in the state and I suppose the world, but there's one thing we're very rich in and that's personalities."

Personalities, characters, eccentrics, fools, misers, indigents—it really doesn't matter what you call them—they are the people who lend themselves to a collection of narratives that furnish the humor endemic to any folk community. Where the local heroes and saints are revered, the local characters are derided, but it is an affectionate derision, one framed more often in mirth than in meanness.

If you hang around Cambridge, Maryland, long enough you're sure to hear of the local tycoon there whose penurious ways turned him into a legendary figure. If you visited him of an evening at his home, so the stories went, after a time he'd ask if you'd object to his turning out the lights; electricity after all was expensive. A bit later he'd comment, "Since we're sitting here in the dark, would you mind if I slipped out of my pants? I don't want to wear them out any sooner than I have to." On the other hand, this was the same man who, when insulted by a clerk in a Salisbury hotel, returned the next week to purchase the entire hotel, just so he could personally fire the offender.

In the days before television took over as the main source of news, the local saloon- or storekeeper often took the role of anchorman and seer in small villages and hamlets. He was always abreast of the local news since he heard versions of it night after night, and if he had any charisma at all, he frequently became a kind of institution himself. Ike Morgan of Klondike rose to such status. He ran a village watering hole called The House of Morgan, and his witty responses to customers became his trademark. Asked if he'd ever been to Hollywood to try his luck, Ike replied, "Why the hell should I go to Hollywood? There I'd be fool among kings. Here I'm a king among fools."

Ike's philosophy inevitably spilled over into politics. When Governor Lane ran the state of Maryland, he signed a sales tax bill that did not sit well with Ike. Ike placed a glass jar on his bar with a sign pasted to it: YOU FEED THE SON-OF-A-BITCH. THESE PENNIES ARE NOT FOR NEW HIGHWAYS, THEY'RE FOR CROOKED LANES.

One day when he was over in Frostburg, a friend asked him how things were going back in Klondike. "Why," said Ike, "things are so slow over there the creek only runs three times a week." One winter a customer inquired if it had been cold out Ike's way. "Cold?" observed Ike, "Why it's been so cold over there that one morning I went out to check the thermometer and there the damn thing was, running up and down the side of the house to keep warm." (A similar response is hung on "Old Willie" Ford of Crisfield. Asked one winter morning if it had "blowed" over his way last night, Willie responded, "Blow? My good Lord, I guess it did blow. I looked over from the bed and it had whitecapped the piss pot.")

Ike and his wife Mag never got on, but there was a good deal of humor that sprang from their relationship.

> When Ike first got married he promised he'd take Mag on a honeymoon to Niagara Falls. Well, Ike was working in the mines then and he couldn't get any time off. But Mag kept nagging at him for promising her a honeymoon and then backing out. So finally Ike got tired of listening to her and told her to go up there by herself. He told her to send along a telegram when she was coming back and he'd come meet her in Cumberland.
>
> Well, after a time Ike got the telegram. (This was back in the days before they had cars.) He had a buckboard but he didn't have a horse so he borrowed a stallion from a neighbor and set out to get Mag.
>
> When they got almost to Cumberland, they passed this surrey with two mares pulling it. That old stallion just reared up on its hind legs and wouldn't budge an inch past those mares.
>
> So Ike got down from the buckboard and got that horse by the harness and held him real tight and looked him in the eye and said, "Now listen here, who got that telegram, you or Ike Morgan?"

Later when Ike had a scrap with his wife, she got so furious she left home to go back and live with her mother. As she coursed out the front door, Ike worried her: "I'll have another woman in this house before the trail you leave going out is cold." Since her mother lived just across the way, Mag kept a keen eye on the place and sure enough that afternoon she noticed a woman sweeping off the porch. She dashed over, burst into the house, only to find Ike himself in one of her own dresses, sitting at the dinner table eating a can of sardines.

Ike always complained that one reason he and his wife never got on was because other women were always after him.

> Now, Ike told this one on himself. Said he was leading this hog home one time and he had this rope tied around one of his front feet. So pretty soon this woman came along and jabbered something to Ike and then she said, "Now don't you molest me."
>
> He said, "How the hell can I molest you and hold this hog at the same time?"
>
> She said, "Well here—I'll hold the hog."

Beside women, it was alcohol that frequently got the best of Ike Morgan, though he'd never admit it. Accosted dead drunk, he'd say he was deathly ill with neuralgia. After a while Mag got sick and tired of Ike coming home drunk all the time so she dressed her brother up like the devil, hid him in some bushes near the house, and told him to give Ike a good scare. When Ike came reeling up the lane that evening, the brother jumped out of the underbrush and hollered, "OOOOHHHH, OOOOHHHH, I'm the devil, I'm the devil."

Ike took one look at him and said, "Well, I'll be damned. I'm glad to meet you. Come on up to the house; I married your sister."

On a near par with Ike Morgan was Rabbit Allen of Eckhart. He was the town's free spirit, a man simple yet wise and he knew better than most how to get something for nothing. When approached by the conductor on the streetcar bound for Frostburg, Rabbit fumbled through his pockets in a very deliberate manner, first the trousers, then the coat, then the vest. When he couldn't find anything, he began the process again. By the time the conductor signalled the motorman to stop the car and let Rabbit off, they were already in Frostburg.

Rabbit always made the best of any situation. When he came home one night to find every bed in the house taken, he took a match, touched off the curtains, and cried "FIRE, FIRE" at the top of his lungs. The family sprang to and put out the blaze while Rabbit fell into the nearest bed. Another time when he tumbled off a roof during a shingling job, a passing neighbor ran over to see if he was all right.

"Are you hurt, Rabbit," he said, "are you hurt?"

"No, I don't think so," he said, "I'm all right. I had to come down for more nails anyway."

On one of the few occasions when Rabbit had money— he'd just received a large insurance check—he walked into the local pub. At the bar he spoke expansively: "When Rabbit drinks, everybody drinks," and the bartender served drinks all around. Then Rabbit reached into his pocket, drew out a dime, and placed it on the counter. Again he spoke expansively: "When Rabbit pays, everybody pays," and he walked out of the saloon. Yet even with his eccentric ways and his continual impoverishment, Rabbit's style caught the attention of the town fathers. One of Frostburg's most prominent businessmen spoke this modest eulogy:

> A number of people have come to me and asked me why I tolerate Rabbit and continue to shower him with handouts. The answer is simple: I'm not giving him anything; he's giving me. There are very few books that I could read that would give me the satisfaction that I get from the few moments of my time I spend with Rabbit. That man could have been anything he had a mind to, but he didn't have the mind to and it doesn't really make any difference.
>
> With all the wealth I may leave behind, it will never be as rich as the wealth that Rabbit leaves behind. My wealth, in time, will be made over; his can never be made over.

Fred Merrbaugh also came from the western part of Maryland, from Lonaconing. People knew him best for the foolish remarks he sometimes uttered. When a man gave him a wild ride in his car the one mile between Pekin and Lonaconing, Fred stepped out of the car, shook himself off, and said to the driver, "By God, the next time I ride down here I'll walk!" Faced with some enormous grapefruits on a vegetable stand in the local store, Fred remarked, "I'll tell you one thing: It wouldn't take many of them things to make a dozen." One evening Fred came home from the mines to find nothing for supper that pleased him. He glanced into the skillet and said, "My God, woman, there ain't enough ham in there to make a cheese sandwich." Another local character from Frostburg also had trouble with his meals:

> Now Old Man Coke, he used to live across the main street from Shupe's Drug Store. They always said he was the contrariest man in Frostburg. Well, anyway, one day he was up the street talking to some friends and the noon bell sounded. He turned to these fellows and said, "I think I'll go home now. If dinner isn't ready, I'll raise hell, and if it is, I won't eat any of it."

Other towns in western Maryland produced characters with any number of odd traits. Andy House never got associated too much with any one place; he moved too often. He always had a railroad ticket in his pocket, and word had it that any time Andy approached the chicken coop, the chickens simply lay on their backs with their legs in the air ready to be tied up for moving. In Lonaconing, John Felder and his wife lived down near the South Branch of the Potomac River. They never kept a very clean house. A friend dropped by one day and noticed a loaf of fresh bread rising on the window sill. "My," he observed, "that's some fine raisin bread you got there."

"That ain't no raisin bread," John's wife said, and she went over, shooed off the flies, and stuck it in the oven.

Dutch Henry Wiegant lived in Frostburg for years and years. He was one of the last of the old-time coppersmiths. When his wife finally died, a number of friends came over to pay their respects. One mourner approached Henry:

> "Oh Henry, it's a dreadful thing about your wife."
> "Vell, yes it is, but it could have been vorse."
> "Could have been worse, how's that?"
> "Vell, it could have been me."

Chin Murphy and his wife always felt the pinch. Chin was over in West Virginia one time and his wife sent him a telegram: "Send some money quick, or I'll go to the poorhouse." Chin wired back: "If you can put off till Saturday, I'll be home and we can go together."

A similar tale got hung on "Pilgrim" Marsh of Smith Island. As a young man he went on the road and it wasn't long before he went completely broke. He wrote home to his father, Charlie:

Dear Dad:
Please send ten dollars. I'm on the hog.

Pilgrim

His father wrote back:

Dear Pilgrim:
You say you're on the hog. Well, ride the son-of-a-bitch home.

Charles

Bill Tyler was a letter writer as well. He trapped muskrats one season down on Jenkins Creek and he bought twenty-four traps from Sears. After a while they started writing him letters trying to get him to pay for the traps, but the Easton man who bought his skins had not paid Bill what he owed him. One day Bill walked into the local store and the storekeeper handed him yet another letter from Sears. He grabbed an old paper bag off the shelf, sat down, and wrote:

Dear Sears:

You're there and I'm here.
They owe me, and I owe thee.
When they pay me, I'll pay thee.
If they don't pay me, I won't pay thee.
Don't write me any more letters.

Sincerely,

Bill Tyler

After that, Sears left him alone.

Ware Evans lived in Rhodes Point on Smith Island. He had considerable intelligence, all right, read a lot of books, and philosophically he seemed sound enough, but when it came to working on the water, he lacked a certain practicality. When his engine failed to run one morning, he knelt down and prayed, "Look, Lord, I've got up early just so I can get down to the fishing ground before anyone else. Please let this engine go." It didn't catch. After several more requests and no luck, he looked up to heaven and said, "Lord, I'm just going to ask you one more time."

Late on a hot summer afternoon a friend met Ware poling his boat back up the creek toward town. He asked him what the matter was.

"Nothing. I put about a gallon and a half of gas in her and it's all used up."

"Well, don't you have any more?"

Yep, but I'm damned if I'm gonna humor her anymore today."

In Marion, Jack Beall never had a dime to his name. One afternoon he was discussing the economic situation in the country with Bob Whittington, a well-heeled businessman.

"Mr. Bob, it ain't fair; you've got all the money and I ain't got any."

"Well, Jack, what do you think we ought to do about it?"

" 'Vide it up."

"But Jack, if we divided it up, at the end of the year I'd have it all back again. What would we do then?"

" 'Vide it up again."

Jack did in fact always seem to have a way of getting in the last word. When Tony Green shot Tom Shelton for chasing his wife, they laid Shelton away in the local cemetery with a fancy inscription above him.

Remember friends as you pass by,
As you are now so once was I,
As I am now you soon shall be,
Prepare in death to follow me.

Jack was a longtime friend of Tony's, so one night he took a crayon and stuck two lines onto the epitaph:

Where you are now I cannot tell,
But I'll bet five dollars you've gone to hell.

Crisfield also had its cast of colorful personalities. So superstitious was Bob Taylor that stories about his antics passed into local legend. Bob would pay a Negro man to come to his house seconds after midnight on New Year's Day, so he wouldn't have to face the bad luck of a woman being the first person at his door. Bob packed crabs for a living and he did very well, but he attributed his success to certain rituals he performed each day to help see him through. In his office no one used his phone in the morning before he did, nor did anyone lay a hand to his personal hatchet before he used it. And each morning before he went to work, Bob Taylor stood on the wharf at Crisfield, looked west, and very ceremoniously saluted Smith Island, the place where he was born.

Leff Webb was a Crisfield butcher and he and his wife had nine children. One Sunday he took them on a boat excursion and when they returned to shore he counted them, one to nine, as they got off off the boat. Suddenly a young woman rushed up to Leff and insisted he had one of her children. "Madam," said Leff, "it doesn't really matter; I came with nine and I'm going home with nine."

Eccentrics frequently intrigue the youth in a community and color the narratives of young storytellers. For years "The Catwoman" lived alone in a rundown mobile home beside the railroad tracks outside Thurmont. More than two dozen cats ran wild in and out of her quarters, and everything about the Catwoman seemed a touch peculiar and mysterious. No one really knew how she had come to this particular station in life, but some said she had once been married to a railroad tycoon who left her when she began to collect cats. Whatever the case, her strange behavior had begun to link her with the occult, at least in the eyes of the local teenagers.

In similar fashion, several generations ago, Graveyard Annie and Joe Brant captured youthful imaginations around Cumberland with their odd mannerisms. Annie never ap-

76

peared in anything but black, making her trek each day to the cemetery. Her husband's death years before initiated the daily pilgrimage, and once at the graveyard she would sit for hours by his gravesite, at times picking flowers off other graves to decorate his. Joe Brant was born at the end of the nineteenth century, the son of a railroad man who died when his son was an infant. To hear the townspeople speak of him, Joe had a variety of talents: artist, musician, mechanic, arsonist. He seldom dressed conventionally, choosing to wear a coat/sweater with a vest underneath and a skull cap with red and white lights which blinked on and off. When saluted on the street Joe countered with an American Indian greeting. Apparently, the man had the speed of a deer and he always raced the Capitol Limited when it pulled out of the Cumberland station for Baltimore. The distance from the station to the viaduct was about half a mile and Joe won every time, hands down. A Cumberland woman said she had seen Joe actually jump over an automobile, but there was no one else around at the time to verify it. One night people in the neighborhood complained of fiddle music coming out of a tree and called the police. When they arrived, they found it was only Joe delivering a serenade, and they let him go.

Like any other folk community, the college campus produces its own set of characters, be they absentminded professors or dumb athletes, and tales about them linger on long after they have left the campus. Back in the Ice Age when I was an undergraduate at Middlebury College we had a remarkable English professor named R. L. Brown. Beowulf, we called him. He was a huge hulk of a man with a deeply furrowed face who chain-smoked while he lectured (never with a note) and his knowledge ran very deep. In the classics of literature course I took, Brown ranged eclectically over every possible subject with a facility of recall that dazzled us. And to argue with the man was futile. In debate his mind was like a giant clamp.

Yet, curiously enough, in the course of his own education Brown had never received the doctoral degree. The master's degree, yes, but not the Ph.D. Around campus the story circulated that a young coed (that's what we called female students back in the fifties) had once approached the great man and

One of the practitioners of screen painting, a seventy-five-year-old Baltimore tradition, is octagenarian Johnny Eck, shown here explaining his techniques to a film crew. (Photograph by Elaine Eff, courtesy of the Painted Screen Society of Baltimore, Inc.)

asked him, "How is it, Professor Brown, that with your remarkable fund of knowledge and your incredible turn of mind you never received the Ph.D.?"

With that Brown drew himself up to his full height, looked down at the young woman, and said, "Who would test me?"

When I first heard this tale, I believed it implicitly. It fit the man perfectly and seemed eminently plausible. Not until years later after I became a folklorist did I realize that what I had then taken for fact was nothing more than an academic folktale, one which flitted from campus to campus getting pinned on the appropriate professor. I discovered that it was a story told for years at Harvard about George Lyman Kitteredge, himself a campus legend and one of the great minds of his time. He, too, lacked the Ph.D.

As a folk character on campus, the dumb athlete vies formidably with professorial types for a place in college legendry, and his stunts still fertilize the accounts of undergraduates long after his four- (or five- or six-) year stint at the school is over. At the University of Maryland, Big Julian was such a figure. He attended the university in the early 1960s, but stories about his antics were still in fashion ten years later. Julian played football and drank prodigious quantities of beer. He stood little on protocol. He awakened a hallmate by plunging his fist through the sleeping student's wall. Once when irritated, he grabbed his tormenter and held him above his head with one hand until he whimpered for mercy. One terrified undergraduate jumped out a second-story window to escape Julian's drunken rage.

On a binge in Atlantic City Julian cut a wide swath. The police needed five patrolmen to subdue him, and even when they got the handcuffs on him, he tore them apart as though they were cobwebs. He returned to College Park from that adventure somewhat bruised and scarred, but with his reputation much inflated. He added to that reputation at a subsequent birthday party.

> I remember one time he came into my room and he looked like he'd put his head inside a washing machine. He had big welts on his ear and stitches on his head and it was all shaved in places. And he comes in and says, "I had a birthday party last night."
>
> So I said, "What did you do, Jules, tame lions?"

79

Come to find out these guys had given him a birthday party down at one of the bars and they gave him a whole keg of beer to drink. He got drunk out of his mind, somebody gave him some lip, and he attacked them, apparently violently enough so that they called the cops. They came in there and they took Jules and this other kid down to the police station and when they were booking them, the kid gave Jules some more lip and Jules went after him again and it took two firemen and five policemen to get him off that kid. They beat the hell out of him with their nightsticks and finally got him into a cell for the night.

Though the police seem to have continuously interrupted Big Julian at his brawling, there is no indication that anyone came upon him reading a book or burning the midnight oil over some deep problem in engineering. No, Julian's star rose in campus legendry because he indulged in activities composed of characteristics on which a good deal of legendry is built: violence and lawlessness. His arena was somewhat different from that of other folk heroes, but the process that developed him as a part of the local folklore was no different from that which shaped Lickin' Bill Bradshaw or Davy Crockett or even Jesse James.

4. Urban Legends

ONE CATEGORY of legend that has received considerable recognition of late and really deserves a chapter all its own is the urban belief tale or legend. Jan Brunvand has dealt with these narratives in three books: *The Vanishing Hitchhiker*, *The Choking Doberman*, and *The Mexican Pet*. Presently, I am told, Brunvand runs a syndicated newspaper column on the subject, but I have never actually picked up a paper where his column appeared. Yet the scope of his attention to this current type of folklore says something about the pervasiveness of the genre and the fascination it holds for the general public. When a form such as the urban legend fixes itself this firmly in American culture, it is up to the folklorist to find out why. Urban legends differ from the other legends in this book, for their attachments lie in the modern urban/suburban corridor, the world of fast-food joints, automobile dealers, hairdressers, department store chains, teenage "parking" grottoes. And the people (or perhaps we should say the victims) we meet wandering through these stories are just the ordinary Joan or John you might meet in the course of an average day: teenage lovers, toll collectors, service station attendants, college students, grandmothers. These tales take place in a recent time frame. Unlike the "once upon a time" fairy tale, which is really set beyond real time, we have the impression that the urban legend could have taken place last week or yesterday. What's more, it's hard to disbelieve these accounts when we know they are attested to by such credible folks as "my sister's boyfriend," or "a good buddy of my brother-in-law's." Very real people pass these accounts on, very real people dwell inside them, and very real people like you and me quite often believe them.

81

Here, for example, is one such story told about a fast-food place in the Washington/Silver Spring area.

> Two couples stopped one night at a notable carryout for a fried chicken snack. The husband returned to the car with the chicken snack. While sitting there in the car eating their chicken, his wife said, "My chicken tastes funny." She continued to eat and continued to complain.
>
> After a while the husband said, "Let me see it." The driver of the car decided to cut the light on and then it was discovered that the woman was eating a rodent, nicely floured and fried crisp. The woman went into shock and had to be rushed to a hospital. It was reported that the husband was approached by lawyers representing the carryout and offered the sum of $35,000. The woman remained on the critical list for several days. Spokesmen from the hospital would not divulge the facts about the case and nurses were instructed to keep their mouths shut. And it was also reported that a second offer was made for $75,000, and this, too, was refused. The woman died, and presumably the case will come to court.

As is easy to see, this tale, which was told by a federal government employee, has all the earmarks of a legend. It gets pinned on a specific place, and as subsequent conversation with the informant disclosed, the actual place was a well-known dispenser of a special brand of fried chicken. Most important, the incident was related as fact. The narrator acknowledged that her brother-in-law actually knew a nurse in the hospital where the woman was taken. (This is frequently the pattern with this type of story: The narrator tries to enlist the audience's gullibility by citing an identifiable source as being in some way connected with the event. I have had students every so often who were so convinced of their accounts because their "uncle" or "stepfather's best friend" had been involved or "seen it in the paper" that they have bet on the truth of the tale. Yet when asked to produce the document or the source, they have come up short.)

Although, according to the storyteller, this particular "fried chicken" event took place in the summer of 1970, the legend still circulates, moving from one location to another, almost always told on the same fast-food chain. There are, of course, variations. In some versions the woman doesn't die from shock as is the case here. Some tales suggest that the rat was in the food because the place had recently been fumigated and one of the poisoned rats had fallen into the batter and been fried up by mistake. In one account, the woman knows she has taken a bite out of a rat when she sees a tail hanging down from her chicken. Different occupational groups further vary things with their own professional twists. In a version heard in one of the Washington law offices from a Justice Department attorney, the emphasis is not so much on the gruesome predicament of eating a rat as on the ramifications of the pending lawsuits.

Stories about food aberrations in restaurants and dining places are nothing new. Odd things like pigeons and cats have been supposedly served up in Chinese restaurants for years, and large-scale pizza delivery operations have been accused of sending out their order with bloody bandages set among the pepperoni. On college campuses, students claim that lab rats turn up from time to time at dinner tables in the refectories, and students (at least the University of Massachusetts) comment derisively about their food in that most common of written folklore forms, the graffito. "Flush twice," read the scratchings over the toilets in more than one campus dormitory, "it's a long way to the dining commons."

It is virtually impossible to know whether the event at the chicken carryout place that spawned the legend ever actually occurred. Let's put it this way: It could have, but it certainly never happened at all the places the stories attest to. Yet we can see the seeds of possibility for this sort of thing when we discover an article such as this in the Washington *Post* (February 3, 1971).

A 76-year-old Falls Church man was awarded $20,000 in damages yesterday on his claim that he was "permanently sickened" by drinking a bottle of Coca-Cola that contained part of a mouse.

George Petalas was awarded the settlement by a Fairfax County Circuit Court jury, which debated for two hours.

In his suit, Petalas claimed that he bought a 10-cent bottle of Coca-Cola on March 20, 1969 from a vending machine in a Safeway Store at 3109 Graham Rd., Falls Church.

He took two swallows in the presence of a store employee, William Wheeler, Petalas said, when he noticed a "strange taste." He and Wheeler then went outside the store and poured the rest of the bottle on the driveway, Petalas testified. At the bottom, Petalas contended, were the back legs and tail of a mouse.

Petalas was hospitalized for three days at Arlington Hospital following the incident, he testified. He alleged through his attorney, Robert J. Arthur, that he has since been unable to eat meat, and has lived on a diet of grilled cheese, toast, and noodles . . .

It is not hard to see how this kind of a report could easily work its way into a verbal rendition, and once it has, the story becomes susceptible to all kinds of changes. I have heard this "mouse in the Coke bottle" yarn in any of a number of versions both before and after I read this newspaper article. One wonders if the bored Coca-Cola plant worker hadn't heard the tale as well and said to himself, "Hmmm, I think I'll set the hind end of reality onto that old wives' tale," and put the mouse where it didn't belong. As the newspaper account went on to report, the bottle company's lawyer testified that the mouse could only have gotten into the bottle through "tampering."

More wishful thinking than tampering is at work in a story like this one told on a well-known department store chain in the greater Washington area:

> This happened to my girlfriend's sister-in-law. One day she was shopping at Klein's department store in Greenbelt. She saw some sweaters that were on sale and tried some on. She felt this prick on her arm but thought it was just a tag. Anyway, she continued shopping. Later in the day her arm started itching. It swelled up and got real red. By evening she felt faint. Her husband took her to the hospital where she was listed in serious or critical condition. They completely retraced her steps that day to try and find out what happened to her. Come to find out it was from that prick from the sweaters. The sweaters had been imported from Japan. Somehow a snake got into them and started a nest. The eggs had hatched and there were tiny snakes in some of the sweaters.

In this story, which has circulated around Maryland and throughout the country, variation once again marks it as a bona fide folktale. In the Maryland accounts, the victim is anyone from "the wife of a man who works in my husband's office" to

84

"a friend of Virginia Spalding's." The snakes are seldom defined as other than "poisonous" except in two versions where they become baby cobras. Storytellers have the sweaters made always in Far Eastern countries—Japan, Vietnam, or China—a clear indication of the Westerner's suspicion (and fascination) with that part of the world. In the western stereotype, the Far East is a mysterious place, a land of yellow rivers, opium dens, occult reckonings, and it breeds a race that bears watching. So it hardly seems odd that wool from such a place might very well hide something as sinister as poisonous snakes. It's the same process of stereotyping that makes Westerners suspect Far Eastern food. We look at that mysterious dish before us and think, my God, that could be almost anything—cat, pigeon, dog. It's a sad commentary on the stereotyping process, but as we know, stereotyping is at the heart of a great deal of folklore.

What strikes me as astonishing in both the carryout and Klein's story is the gullibility of "the folk." Faced with documented proof that no such event ever occurred, people still believe it. As soon as these stories began turning in the rumor mills, both organizations denied explicitly that any such event had ever taken place. In fact, they made statements to the local newspapers that the stories were without foundation. The Washington *Star* carried two articles on the Klein incident. In the first (February 13, 1969), entitled "No Snakes in Sweaters; The Tale is Just a Yarn," they reported that a thorough check of both department stores and hospitals had turned up no evidence to support the story. Ten days later the same paper printed another article that drew attention to their first report and said that since it had appeared, calls to the newspaper about the event had "increased in number—and in certitude." The folk obviously will not let go of something they want to believe.

Why such tenacity? By and large the accounts focus on large chain operations like department stores or fast-food places, outfits that mass-produce goods the average suburbanite has been conditioned to think he cannot do without. More frustrating still, these are conglomerates over which the consumer has little control—unless it is through a derogatory tale that might derail business for a time. There is evidently a

85

lot of wishful thinking going on here: This is made clear when several informants reveal that—due to a decrease in business caused by the incident—the company is unable to meet its payroll and may have to close down.

This same process bears directly on the widely told legend of "the death car" that gets attached to a not-so-popular secondhand car dealership in the Washington suburbs. There is no doubt about this storyteller's point of view.

> You know that car dealer out on University Boulevard? Its specialty is repossessed cars. Well, they say they repossessed this red Corvette a few years ago. The owner had been murdered and hidden in the trunk. Well, this car dealer cleaned up the car, repainted it and recarpeted the trunk, and about a week later they sold that car to some guy. But he returned the car after a week, said there was a bad smell in it he couldn't get rid of. This happened a couple of more times with other people who bought the car, and now the dealer is stuck with the car. I think the going price is something like $100. But it serves them right. The place is a big clip joint anyway. I hope they never sell the car.

In a culture where the automobile is such an absolute in both real life and advertisements, it's not surprising to find the car as a pivotal factor in much of modern legendry. Vehicles enable teenagers the mobility and escape they so desperately covet. This release in turn allows them to discover out-of-the-way places where they can carry on amorous adventures. Yet as these two widely disseminated stories suggest, all kinds of anxieties lie right outside the car window.

From Leonardtown:

> There was a couple parked out on a lonely road down near the river. The girl and her boyfriend ran out of gas or something happened to the car. The boy left to go to get help. The girl fell asleep on the seat and one time she woke during the night and she thought she heard scratching on the roof of the car, but she didn't think anything of it. She thought it was just some twigs and since she didn't have a watch, she didn't have any idea what time it was. She thought maybe he had just left. The next thing she knows it's morning and there's a police of-

ficer near her car. He woke her up and said, "Miss, please get out of the car and walk to the police car but don't look back." But as she was walking to the police car, her curiosity got the best of her and she turned around and looked back. And hanging from a tree by his feet was her boyfriend and he looked like he'd been slit. His clothes were all in rags and he was bleeding. He was dead. What she heard during the night were his fingernails scratching on the roof of the car.

I also heard in connection with this that there was supposedly a "Hook Man" running around in the area. Several people had told stories about this in reference to the "Hook Man." Everyone supposed it was the "Hook Man" who had done this.

From Baltimore:

This story happened on Clyburn [sic] Lane in Baltimore near the mental institution there. One night a couple was out on a date. The girl was arguing with her date because he wanted to "park" and she refused to. He drove her to Clyburn Lane and parked the car. She kept telling him that it wasn't safe. She wanted to go home. Her boyfriend said that all the car doors were locked. While listening to the radio they heard a news flash that a patient had escaped from the institution near there. He was a dangerous rapist and could be identified by a hook on his left arm in place of the hand. The girl was frightened and started crying. The boy floored the gas pedal and zoomed away. They didn't talk the whole way home. When the boy got to the girl's house, he went around to the other side of the car to let her out and there was a hook hanging on the door handle.

These two tales have gained enough national recognition that folklorists have given them actual names: "The Murdered Boyfriend" and "The Hook." In fact one scholar has even subjected "The Hook" to a heavy-handed Freudian analysis in which the the hooked arm becomes a phallic symbol which the female subconsciously wishes ripped away. More interesting perhaps is that in the first account the hook man gets blamed for the deed, a process quite common in folklore and one which in many ways made folk heroes out of figures like Robin Hood and Jesse James: Give a dog a bad name and he kills every sheep in the land.

Another tale frequently related at teenage gatherings also deals with young people and cars. A Baltimore woman recalled this, which she had heard at a party:

> There was this girl and one night she was driving back here to Baltimore by herself and before she got to town she had to go through this very sparsely populated area. Well, pretty soon she noticed that there was this truck following her and every once in a while for no reason this truck would throw its high beam lights on her. She got pretty nervous while this continued and so, when she reached a more populated area in the suburbs of Baltimore, she pulled over to the curb, jumped out of the car and started running for the nearest house. The truck pulled up right behind her and a fellow jumped out and yelled to her that he wasn't after her, just trying to protect her.
>
> Come to find out that in the back of the girl's car was this killer, and every time he rose up to grab her, this truck driver flashed on his lights and he'd drop back down behind the seat.

Other accounts portray the girl's deliverer as a gas station attendant who spies the killer crouched behind the seat of the car as he fills the gas tank. On a lame pretext, he suggests that the girl come into the station building, but it is late at night and she is understandably reluctant to do so. Finally she does and so learns about her passenger.

Legends such as this frequently become didactic devices. I remember a number of years back I had a student come up after a class during which I'd referred to this particular story. She had a very disillusioned look on her face and I soon found out why. Shortly after she'd gotten her driver's license her mother had told her this story about the killer in the backseat as absolute fact and as a stern admonition on why you should always check behind the seat before you get in to drive any car.

The automobile surfaces as a key accessory in many other narratives and teenage jokes. Medical students regale their friends with the account of their compatriots who secure the arm of a cadaver, glue a fifty-cent piece to the fingers, and then

88

drive to the Baltimore tunnel where they release the coin and the arm to the astounded tollbooth attendant. In some versions, the man's hair turns completely white from fright, in others he is committed to a mental institution.

Similar for its prankish quality is a story I heard when I was in college back in the late 1950s. Then I believed it implicitly; now as a folklorist I see it has all the earmarks of an apocryphal tale. A group of Yale undergraduates, or so the account went, commandeered three trucks, a half-dozen jackhammers, picks, shovels, and other implements, purchased hard hats and uniforms, and took off for New York City. They cordoned off a good section of Broadway and went to work tearing up the street with their equipment. Come quitting time, they threw all their gear back into the trucks, took down their cordon, and returned to New Haven, leaving the city with a $50,000 repair job.

Likewise, stories such as the one about the grandmother's corpse and the naked man in the trailer could not very well be told without the automobile as an accessory. A family on a car trip vacation take the grandmother along only to have her die in a remote location. They wrap up the corpse and strap it to the roof. On their return they stop at a restaurant for breakfast and while there the car is stolen along with the grandmother. The family then has all kinds of problems trying to probate the will without a body. In the other story, a man and his wife are traveling with a trailer. One hot day while the wife is driving, her husband strips down in an effort to cool off. When the vehicle lurches away from an intersection, he is thrown abruptly out the back and left at a crossroads in the middle of nowhere with nothing on.

Doubtless the best known of these modern legends dealing with the automobile is the ubiquitous tale of "The Ghostly Hitchhiker." But unlike many of the others, this story has roots that date back to the horse and buggy era. Maryland narrators place the event in various locations. A Salisbury man, who came originally from West Virginia, hung the tale on a personal friend of his:

> Now this was supposed to have happened to Doc Smith, a fellow who taught with me the second year I taught at Ridgeley

High School. Doc's father was a druggist at the time in Philip-
pi, West Virginia.

Now Doc, or young Doc, this is, was on his way back from driving to Parsons one night and he was coming along this mountain
road. Of course, it was a hard-paved road and all that, but all at
once he saw this girl standing right at the curve in the road,
hitchhiking. So he picked her up and drove her home. She
directed him to where her home was.

So being polite, when they got there he got out and went
around to open the door for her. He said when he got around to
her side of the car, she was gone. Well, he thought she'd probably got out of the car and gone into the house, but he said he
didn't know how in the world she could have got in there that fast.

So Doc went up and knocked on the door. And the mother
came to the door and said, "Yes?"

Doc said, "Does your daughter—I think I had your daughter in
the car with me and I went around the car to let her out and she
was gone. Did she come in here, into the house?"

The mother said, "You're not the first one that this has happened to. My daughter was killed four years ago there on that
same curve where you picked her up. "

In other parts of Maryland the tale takes on a number of variations. In a Cumberland accounting the driver is a taxi-cab hack;
in a Crisfield rendition, he is a traveling salesman and the place
he picks up the ghost is called, appropriately enough, Dead
Man's Corner. Scholars who have studied this migratory
legend on an international scale have found it in oral tradition
in such far-flung places as China, Turkey, and Hawaii (where
the driver is a rickshaw hack). Some versions append a coda
that simply convinces the driver that he has, without question,
taxied a ghost. On the way home the girl becomes chilled and
requests a garment. The driver lends her his sweater. When he
tells the parents this, they take him next day to the cemetery
and there, wrapped around the girl's headstone, he finds his
sweater.

In studying these urban legends one soon becomes aware
that the majority of them lodge in the repertoires of teenagers.
Adults tell them, certainly, but generally the subject matter ap-

peals to youthful imaginations. There are, for instance, a number of stories that have to do with babysitting, a teenage profession that for many young people becomes the first real responsibility that entails possible danger and anxiety. We can imagine young girls at a slumber party trying to better one another with their babysitting escapades and in the process employing more traditional stories to tantalize their audience. In time, these same teenagers move on to college. The late night dormitory room replaces the slumber party and we get a well-known story like this from a University of Maryland student:

> These two girls were staying alone in a college dorm over a vacation and they heard that an axe murderer was on the loose. One of the girls was afraid to stay alone in her room, but she couldn't talk her friend into staying with her because her friend thought it was stupid. Her friend told her to lock the door and then she left. A little while after that the girl heard a scratching on her door. She was scared to death so she didn't open the door. At dawn the noise stopped and she opened the door. There was her friend with an axe sticking out of her head. She had met the murderer halfway down the hall and had crawled back and had been scratching for help.

This tale gets told in a variety of ways on college campuses all over the country and has, in at least one instance, captured the credibility of an entire town. I first published versions of this legend in book form back in 1971. In 1986 just before Halloween I got a call at the University of Massachusetts from a newspaper reporter in Sunbury, Pennsylvania. She told me that in her region there was a story going around that people were beginning to take quite seriously. According to one version of the tale, a psychic had recently appeared on NBC's "Today Show" and predicted that on Halloween a mass murder would occur in a cemetery overlooking a university. More to the point, the murders would take place at a university which shared the same name with a nearby river, and the university, the river, and the town where this would happen all began with the letter "S." A great many people thought this unlucky event was destined to make news in Selinsgrove, a town on the Susquehanna

91

River, home of Susquehanna University. This young reporter said she had read something I had written on urban legends years before and wanted to know if I cared to comment on this story.

The whole thing didn't suprise me very much, I told her. Her community had simply been taken in by a broadly based story cycle. I pointed out to her that four or five years before on the University of Massachusetts campus a similar rumor had run wild. On Halloween eve, so the prediction went (and it had been predicted by no less an authority than Jeane Dixon), an axe murderer would kill a female student on a large university campus in western Massachusetts. Since the University of Massachusetts is the only large school in the western part of the state, the prediction really took hold, and one sorority actually canceled a Halloween party they had scheduled for that evening.

Beyond college at professional schools legends persist that frequently draw on old thematic material. Here, for example, is a tale told among medical students:

There was a doctor who worked in a Baltimore hospital and he was always playing practical jokes. His girlfriend was a nurse in the hospital and she had a roommate. The doctor and the nurse decided to play a practical joke on the roommate who was also a nurse on the opposite shift. They took an arm the doctor had amputated and hung it on a string hanging from a light in the ceiling, so that when the roommate grabbed the light cord she would grab the arm instead. Well, when it came time for the roommate to come on duty, she didn't show up. This kind of bothered the nurse who had helped in the joke, so she called the apartment but no one answered. The nurse and the doctor went to the apartment and found the nurse sitting in the corner, her hair turned completely white, chewing on this arm. The girl had gone stark raving mad and had to be put into an institution. The doctor lost his license and the nurse was fired. Exactly one year later at two different locations, the doctor and the nurse were both involved in accidents in which they lost an arm.

Much teenage activity and interaction, as we know, hinges on acceptance. It is the insider/outsider entanglements that motivate many youthful antics. Built into this acceptance—be it admission to a fraternity or sorority or simply linking up with a youth group—is the whole matter of ritual. You've got to do something to demonstrate your macho mettle, and what you must do is often prescribed by tradition. There is practically always a test involved that allows the group to witness the threshold of your fear, and invariably the test takes place at night in some remote place like a cemetery.

For years in a shadowy corner of the Druid Ridge Cemetery off Reisterstown Road near Baltimore stood a bronze replica of Saint-Gaudens's famous sculpture, The Adams Memorial (often called "Grief"). The artwork depicted a seated woman, heavily veiled, leaning forward in a posture of great emotional torment. At the base of the statue was the single embossed word, "Agnus." It was a very forbidding-looking monument, and it stood in an isolated part of the cemetery. Over time, the teenage folk began to use it for their initiation rites, and they gave it a name—Black Aggie. To gain admittance into whatever group, you had to sit in Black Aggie's lap at midnight. As one might suppose, stories began to circulate about Black Aggie's curse, and the things that had happened to people who had tried the test and failed. Several tales emerged that explained how the statue had become cursed in the first place. One informant believed a man named Mr. Agnus and his wife had been caretakers of the Druid Ridge Cemetery. When she died, he buried her beneath this figure. Within a few years, however, he took up with and married his wife's sister, and at that point his first wife returned from the grave and killed her sister. Both sisters, so this storyteller believed, were buried beneath the statue. On the other hand, a Baltimore informant described Black Aggie as a witch.

> There was a very old religious man named Agnus. He was married to a very haggard woman. In her youth she'd been bad, wanton, you know, and Mr. Agnus never forgave her for that. He even felt that he'd been forced to marry her 'cause she lied and said she was pregnant when she really wasn't. Mr. Agnus felt she had the devil's spirit in her, especially when she grew older. She used to go 'round mumbling to herself

93

and drinking special brews of tea for her ailments. When she was really old she took ill and lay in and out of a coma for several weeks. When she was lying there sick, her limbs jumped and twitched, probably from some sort of muscle contraction. But Mr. Agnus thought she had the devil in her and so when she finally died, he placed the statue on her grave 'cause he knew that an evil spirit couldn't come through metal. He felt that her spirit would be forced to stay underground and he'd be safe.

By far the largest body of tradition surrounding Black Aggie issued from pranks connected with some sort of initiation rite. The pattern predictably followed a set course: The initiate was thoroughly educated in all the traditions surrounding the statue and then told that in order to become a member of the organization he must pass a night in Black Aggie's lap, or look into her eyes at midnight. Of course, the rigors of the exercise only increased when he was told of the two Towson boys who sat in the statue's lap one night. When nothing unaccountable happened, they jeered loudly and jumped back into their car. As they pulled out onto Reisterstown Road a truck plowed them down and they died instantly.

Other accounts held that if you sat in Black Aggie's lap at midnight, her arms would embrace you and squeeze you to death. Steve Bledsoe tried it on fraternity hell night. Just at twelve o'clock his friends who were waiting nearby heard him scream, "It's moving, it's moving!" but fortunately he was able to break loose before the statue got a good grip. Another pledge was not so lucky. His fraternity brothers left him in Aggie's lap all night. When they returned in the morning, his corpse lay at the statue's feet, the hair turned snow white.

There were other casualties as well. One lad, foolish enough to venture into that statue's presence one evening, was discovered the following morning with his face scratched to ribbons. A Timonium man recalled hearing that the local police had discovered the body of yet another boy "mashed to a pulp" lying at Black Aggie's feet. Those unwitting enough to look into the statue's eyes (some said they were emerald, others, that they were ruby red and actually bled at particular hours) were supposedly struck blind in an instant, and a pregnant girl tempted fate when she gazed at Black Aggie, for her child would surely emerge stillborn. The statue caused more than a little consternation with a Cub Scout troop:

> What I heard was that there was this troop of Cub Scouts who decided to camp overnight near the pond in Druid Ridge Cemetery. They had to pass by the statue of Black Aggie in order to get to their campsite.
>
> Well, that night while everyone was asleep, two of the scouts snuck away and went exploring in the cemetery. The scoutmaster woke up after a while and saw that the two boys were missing. He looked all around there and pretty soon he found one of the boys. The kid was hysterical and he couldn't even speak a word. Later they found the body of the other boy and he had a broken neck.
>
> After a few days the first boy got better and he could speak. Now there's a belief that something terrible will happen to you if you go near Black Aggie after midnight. The dead boy knew this, but his friend said he wanted to climb up on the statue anyway. And when he did, the statue actually moved and the boy fell down. The friend said the statue really struck him and killed him, but all the adults said that he'd probably just fallen down. But anyways, there's always been a lot of difference of opinion on this matter.

Clearly the legendary material that most appeals to the teenage folk has more than just a touch of whimsy in it. These storytellers tend towards the Gothic in their accounts, spicing their narratives with blood and violence—shredded faces, pulverized bodies, decapitation. Yet within all of this lore there lurks the shred of possibility that makes a tale hang on. It would not be hard to imagine some youth, filled full of Black Aggie beliefs, forced to sit one night in her lap. He shakes physically in his own corner of terror, but in his mind's eye it is the bronze form that moves beneath him. His fright increases, he faints, falls from the statue, and dies of a broken neck. The adults claim it was only a tumble; the teenagers know better: Black Aggie's curse at work again.

95

Ellen (a pseudonym) is among the western Maryland women who craft rag rugs, domestic items that have roots in pre-Revolutionary times. (Courtesy Geraldine Johnson)

Most of the stories about this statue in the Druid Ridge Cemetery were collected in the late sixties and early seventies. Apparently vandalism to the Saint-Gaudens replica and to the cemetery in general became so severe that in the mid-1970s authorities removed the statue. Unless the teenage folk have found another gravesite to work their mysterious rituals around, Druid Ridge Cemetery has now been left to the dead so far as I know. Yet I am sure that a canvassing of the young people in any community would turn up a similar pattern of stories and rituals that initiate fear and in turn furnish a challenge and some sort of rite. The tensions in the passage from childhood into adult status demand it, and these teenage legends provide a release from those constraints.

In so much of this modern legendry one senses an easy fluidity. Tales move much more rapidly in oral tradition today than they did a century ago. The facility of travel and the pervasiveness of the media see to that. A catchy story or joke can move across the country in the space of an afternoon, and it is not hard to see how the tale about the fried chicken carryout could appear almost anywhere and attach itself to a comparable business enterprise in any suburban community. Here, for example, in this account collected in 1967 is firm evidence not only of this sort of ubiquity, but also of a legend's staying power as well. Though the location and the particulars vary, this same story has been told to me as fact within the last three months.

> When I was fifteen or sixteen years old, bouffant hair styles were very much the rage. It was almost as if it were a contest to see which girl could rat her hair the highest and pour the most spray onto it. One day I went to the beauty shop to have my hair done. My hairdresser told me this story, and she swore that it really happened to a friend of her niece's.
>
> There was this girl who had ratted her hair so high, and put so much hair spray on it, that she never took it down and combed it out or washed it. One day a spider fell into her hair. When the black widow spiders hatched, they bit her scalp and she died. I heard this story all over northern and southern California. When I moved to Baltimore, I met people who had heard the same story.

97

They said it happened to a girl who had been a dancer on the Buddy Dean Show, on Baltimore television. The people said that a bee had gotten into the girl's head and stung her and she died from the bee sting because the doctor couldn't get to her head in time, due to the hair.

Beyond travel and the media, these urban legends last because they employ modern appurtenances that anyone can identify with. Touchstones such as the hairdresser and the car dealer and the department store all generate a framework that adds to a story's credibility. With this sort of legendary accounting going on, it would be folly to count the process of folklore in Maryland dead. On the contrary, it is just as alive as the rat the Baltimore woman brought home from Mexico thinking it was a cute stray dog.

5. Shorter Forms

TRADITIONAL SPEECH AND NAMES

WHETHER WE know it or not, the language we use everyday is often rich in traditional words and phrases that we have unconsciously absorbed. Take, for instance, this conversation between two sorority sisters discussing their spring prom.

Damn, what am I going to do. It's three o'clock and I don't have a date.

What do you mean, you don't have a date? I thought you were going with that awesome bouncer.

He has to work at Barsies tonight.

I can't believe he blew you off; what a loser.

You've got to help me, I need you to set me up.

OK, relax, we can fix you up with a Pike or a Beta.

Well, I want to go with someone hot who I can scoop.

Outsiders might have a bit of trouble set in a room with this kind of language bouncing back and forth. They probably wouldn't know that awesome means handsome, Barsies refers to a bar named Barcellaties, to blow someone off has to do with canceling out at the last moment, a loser is a jerk, Beta and Pike refer to local fraternities, a hot male is one with a good physique, and the verb "to scoop" can mean anything from a kiss to sexual intercourse. The speech of young college women overflows with vocabulary like this. It is what gives their group its identity. In a way their language defines them, as it does all of us.

The difference between the folk speech of an average college student and the members of a more isolated group, say

West Virginia coal miners or Eastern Shore watermen, is that the college student's language changes more rapidly. Every four years the student body at an institution is virtually replaced with new people, but down in a village like Wenona on Deal Island or a hamlet like Lawsonia near Crisfield there is no such turnover, and old speech patterns hold on for a long time. Even the introduction of television, which some fear may one day homogenize us all, seems to have had only a slight effect on language in many of these outlying areas. Linguists tell us that traditional speech does not corrupt easily, which is good news for those who hope to see tradition preserved, bad news for some schoolteachers who would like to see all the aberrational burrs removed from all speech everywhere.

Every group, then, has its own language and speech patterns, and the tighter the group the more salient its argot, at least to the outsider. Though my career profession as a college professor has placed me amid the lingo of the college campus, I have been part of groups like paratroopers and lumbermen for a time, and thus have been introduced to a totally different assortment of terms that I needed to know to get along in these occupations. Jumping out of airplanes for two years back in the early 1950s, I became intimate with words like "streamer" (a parachute which disengages from the backpack but does not open), "straight leg" (a nonjumper), "static line" (line attached to the plane that pulls the parachute loose), "airborne shuffle" (certain step used when moving down the aircraft prior to jumping). Later, working in the woods of Washington state for the Weyerhauser Company, I became familiar with other phrases and names like "choker" and "whistle punk," "haywire," "donkey" and "straw boss," and many many more that have long since lost their way in the occluded memory of a fifty-four-year-old.

In Maryland as a folklorist working to collect material from the Eastern Shore watermen, I recognized at once a group whose speech was framed in a long-standing tradition. Here were people whose roots in some cases went back to Elizabethan England and they frequently used words that caught a greenhorn like myself off guard. When a man spoke of his boat as being "wally" or "cranky," I had no idea what he was talking about and had to ask around to discover that what he meant, in my terminology, was "tender" or "tippy." And a word like "jubrous," once common on Smith Island, had to be explained to me as meaning skeptical. "I'm jubrous about going crabbing, weather like this," a waterman might say on a threatening morning. Many of these words, which strike an off-islander as curious and uncommon, are holdover or "relic" words that have dropped out of conventional speech. Because of the relative isolation of a particular region they hang on and brighten up the conversation.

If you listen to lower Eastern Shore talk for any amount of time, you begin to hear the traditional flavor of the speech surface in three different forms: the dialect, the syntax, and the words and phrases themselves. When I first began to spend time in tiny places like Fairmount and Chance, Rhodes Point, Calvary, and Tylerton I had a devilish time understanding the dialect. At times an interpreter would have helped. I felt a little better when an Englishman who had moved to the Eastern Shore told me whenever he heard a man from Smith Island or Deal Island talk he thought he was right back in a pub in Devon, England. And this makes sense, when you realize that in fact many of the settlers of the lower Eastern Shore came originally from the three southwestern districts of the British Isles: Cornwall, Wales, and Devon.

In the common turn of phrase, one learns that watermen sail "drudge" (dredge) boats when they go "austerin'" (oystering). They haul out their vessels once a year, to get them "corked" (caulked) before they can be "lanched" (launched) again. Out on the Bay the weather is never calm, but "kam" or, to add a touch of embellishment, "slick kam" or "kam as a dish." A steely grey windless day as sometimes comes on in the late fall, older Smith Islanders referred to as "slick slatey" or "slickity slatey." In weather like that there was no need to "heist" (hoist) the sail. You simply lowered the push boat, stuck her nose up under the stern of the "batteau" (skipjack), and headed for the "thurfer" (thoroughfare) beyond the distant "pint" (point) where home was.

Formal grammarians who appreciate correct syntax and the proper agreement of nouns and verbs might wince a bit at

101

some of the sentences that spring from an Eastern Shoreman's tongue. For example, they say "div" for dove, "drownded" for drowned, as in "He div overboard and got drownded." When they make a discovery about something and you ask about it, they preface their explanation with, "How come I to know this was . . ." On the Eastern Shore, "either" invariably means none: "I can feed you dinner, but I don't have either biscuits." To be "up and down" with somebody doesn't designate a stormy relationship, but rather that that particular somebody cannot be found. Hardworking people on the Shore never get tired, they simply "give out." Other traditional alterations produce such anomalies as, "He overed his cold"; "I heard tell of"; "love one or nother"; "I'd like for you to go to the store"; "shut the door to"; "it belongs to be that way." And then there was the good Methodist lady who always sang the line to her favorite hymn the way she thought it should have been written, "Brighten the corner where you're at."

Smith Islanders furnish a number of expressions that spice up their daily conversations. When someone expels gas, he "poots," and he "gaps" when he yawns. Something very flat is "all spreeted out." A "snapper rig" is a makeshift arrangement that might lead one into a "kelter" or a "pretty time" (a bad situation) and bring on a "duck fit" (unpleasant reaction). When a waterman has his engine at full bore, he "really has it on her." And not surprisingly, in a maritime community like Smith Island, seafaring expressions slide over into everyday domestic life. A mother chastises her wayward child with, "Do that again, and I'll flinder your stern" (whip you). One "battens down" the house for a bad blow, just as one "stows" things away in the closet. Ashore a girl never faints, she "keels over," nor does anyone simply leave the island; they "rig up and go."

Alex Kellam remembered the Smith Island expression "sigh," a shortened form of "says I" which was common there at the turn of the century.

> Now for instance, if we were kicking up, my grandfather's uncle would say, "Sigh, boy, sigh, you let me speak to you just one more time." They always said, "sigh." They never said "says I" to you. Said "Sigh, boy, sigh, what are you doing?"

102

And they used that all the time . . . I've heard them all, all my uncles used that. Grandfather, too. I remember it very well now. The women didn't use it but the men did.

In these Eastern Shore communities there is often a reason for some of the localized speech, but only occasionally is there someone old enough to remember what event or activity actually triggered the word or phrase. In the village of Rhodes Point on Smith Island, for instance, they used to speak of "a Rhodes Pointer" and they didn't have in mind a local inhabitant. The term was part of the sailing parlance. Anyone who knows anything about the way of a sailboat knows that to make a good mooring under sail requires considerable skill. Without power, you can't simply drive your boat to the mooring buoy and pick it up. You must sail below or to leeward of your target, gauge your distance and the strength of the wind correctly, and then shove your helm over and shoot up for the mooring. If you're too close when you turn, you'll overshoot and your momentum will carry you by too fast; if you're too far away, your boat will fall off short of your destination. Either way you have to go back and try again. For the neophyte it can be very frustrating. But every Rhodes Point waterman became so adept at shooting his small skipjack up into the wind and having its way die out just as the boat's bow nudged up against the buoy, that "a Rhodes Pointer" became the proverbial expression for a perfect mooring.

Similarly, in the village of Mount Vernon on the mainland, old man Clarence Street lost faith in paper money. He transacted everything with silver and one day he ran an advertisement in the local paper. "Fat hen, 19 cents a pound. All cash, no goat money." Most people have long since forgotten the advertisement, but the term "goat money" still holds for anything phoney. Near Elliott Island Sammy I. lived next door to his brother Lisha. For years they talked about bringing their homes together, but the closest they ever got to it was to lay a board plank between the houses. When solicitors for charity arrived at Lisha's door they were always met with, "Sammy I. pays for all." Once again, the local residents, familiar with the Sammy and Lisha situation, set the retort into oral tradition where it lasted much longer than the characters who spawned it.

Nicknaming is far too often overlooked in folklore. It is a process which, it seems to me, often holds a family or a community together in a very subtle way. It lends a group a certain bond, a bit of esoteric lore that sets it apart and gives it a sense of identity. Nicknames mean little to the outsider. Even though he might be familiar with people in the community on a formal basis, the outsider could sit in on a local gathering where the inhabitants were referring to one another by their nicknames, and be utterly lost. What is more, in tightly knit communities where families have been intermarrying for generations, you will sometimes have eight or nine people with the same name. Nicknaming provides a very functional way of determining who is who. Once more the lower Eastern Shore provides an example with which I am most familiar.

Near the town of Crisfield, the small outlying hamlets that usually comprise a local store, a cluster of homes, and not much else have enough Byrds or Lawsons living in them to become designated Byrdtown and Lawsonia, but they might just as easily have been called Nelsonia or Wardtown for all the Nelsons and Wards who live there. On Smith Island, there are a lot of Bradshaws, Evanses, and Marshalls. Tylers are in good supply and not surprisingly Tylerton, a community at the island's southeast corner, is where you can find a good many of them. Not all these place names appear on road maps, but they are geographical fixtures in the minds and memories of the local inhabitants.

When the roots of these families date back into the eighteenth, sometimes seventeenth, century, a community can produce quite a number of George Lawsons or William Bradshaws over that period of time, and all of them may live within two or three miles of one another. So the folk get around the problem by distinguishing their neighbors with imaginative names such as Coon Zenkins, Mortar Johnny, Graveyard Annie, Ginseng Nash, Scatter Eye Sines, Pilgrim Marsh, Foolish

Bill Williams, Mealbags Lawson, Dragon Nelson, Rooster Riggin, Nimrod Sterling.

Edward "Ham" Tull couldn't remember exactly how he got his own nickname, but he delivered the mail in Lawsonia for years and he swore his job would have been just about impossible without nicknames. In fact, he gave an account that suggested the power of the nicknaming process:

> This fellow come down here from Salisbury. He was delivering something to him [George "Pony" Lawson] or something like that. I don't really remember. But anyway this fellow come up and knocked on the door. Pony comes to the door and says, "Yes, what can I do for you?"
>
> Man said, "I'm looking for a Mr. George Lawson."
>
> He said, "I'm sorry, nobody by that name lives here."
>
> So the fellow turned around and started back for his car, and Pony, he started to go back into the house. And all of a sudden he realized that the fellow was after him. "That's me, I'm George Lawson." He didn't even know his real name, just that name "Pony."

Unlike Tull, most of us can recall the derivation of names we get pinned to us sometime in our lives. In college I was called "Gator" because in my dormitory room freshman year I kept a pet alligator which frightened the hell out of the janitorial staff when the creature periodically came out from beneath my dresser and hissed at them. As you might suppose, the dean put an end to these highjinks in short order. To this day, I don't believe a lot of my old college chums even know my real name, but the nickname and the yarns that go along with it they recall with considerable amusement.

Similarly in Lawsonia two of the Nelson clan, "Bluebird" and "Ducky," remembered where their nicknames came from. As a child, Bluebird's bright blue suit worn on the way to church one Sunday arrested the gaze of an old man who remarked, "Well, will you look, here comes a bluebird." As for Ducky, when he was a kid he used to sneak down into the family duck pen and try to pull the heads off the fowl, much to his

105

parents' dismay. Farther up the Eastern Shore on the Choptank River there was "Snubber" Bennett:

> Ed and Norm Bennett were bringing a little old bugeye loaded with oysters up to Cambridge. They couldn't get her around, so they squared off and took her up where the big ships was. Finally they nosed her in under a high clay bank. Norm was letting out the anchor chain when Ed called, "Snub her."
>
> Norman answered, "Snub her, hell! It's all gone. Three hundred foot of chain and the whole works."
>
> Well, she nosed right into that clay bank and stuck there. They went up a couple of days later and pulled and tugged until they got her out. People used to call out to him after that whenever he came into the store, "Here comes Snubber Bennett."

PROVERBS AND PROVERBIAL SPEECH

Like folk speech, the proverb is tight enough and its content pithy enough to preclude much variation. Moreover, proverbs are sometimes phrased in rhyme ("Haste makes waste") which makes them easier still to remember. Even in our urban/suburban culture, which tends to undermine some of the older forms of folklore, the proverb remains a vital form. I have spoken with more than one college student who recalled older members in their families punctuating a small lesson in penury with, "A penny saved is a penny earned" or "Don't be penny-wise and pound-foolish." A sound yet simple didacticism resides in many of these expressions, which may have been what has enabled them to persist so long. Though some proverbs might appear to contradict one another ("Absence makes the heart grow fonder"; "While the cat's away, the mice will play"), there is enough wit and wisdom expressed in them to have caught the folk imagination. Some proverbs, as can be seen, make their statement in a straight apothegm while others observe a truth metaphorically. The true proverb usually appears in a fixed form ("A stitch in time saves nine") while the proverbial phrase, anthologized in the infinitive ("to fry in hell"), has a certain flexibility when spoken. ("After what he did last night,

I'll bet he's going to fry in hell.") A selected sampling from Maryland includes:

If you run with wolves, you've got to howl.

A barking dog never bites.

Idle hands are the devil's workshop.

A word to the wise is sufficient.

Birds of a feather stick together.

The empty wagon rattles loudest.

Beauty is as beauty does.

A new broom sweeps clean.

An ounce of prevention is worth a pound of cure.

Even a dumb squirrel will find an acorn once in a while.

Every tub has to sit on its own bottom.

Sow your wild oats on Saturday night; then go to church on Sunday and pray for crop failure.

Home is where the heart is.

Promises, like piecrusts, are easily broken.

Where there's smoke, there's fire.

Who knows most, says least.

A constant guest is never welcome.

When an ass goes a-traveling, he never comes back a horse.

Little pitchers have big ears.

You can't teach an old dog new tricks.

Willful waste makes woeful want.

Short accounts make long friends.

In the realm of the blind, the one-eyed are kings.

Life is short and full of blisters.

There are more flies to be caught with honey than with vinegar.

What's good for the goose is good for the gander.

Show me the company you keep, and I'll tell you what you are.

to buy a pig in a poke

to cut your nose off to spite your face

to put your foot in your mouth

to not know your ass from a hole in the ground

to know which side your bread is buttered on

to have champagne tastes with a beer pocketbook

to have a face that would stop a clock

to have something go in one ear and out the other

to put the cart before the horse

Equally as common as proverbial phrases is the proverbial comparison which salts our everyday speech in a variety of delightful ways. These comparisons appear most of the time as straight similes ("as dumb as a meat axe," "as pretty as a robin in a rosebush," "as busy as a bee in a tar bucket"), or in a more comparative form ("so foolish he can't pour piss out of a boot with the directions printed on the heel," "so poor when I was born we had to get the neighbors to have me"). Irony surfaces in many of these phrases. Something can be "as clear as glass," but it can also be "as clear as mud" and a bald man can be "as hairy as a doorknob." The proverbial comparison at times provides images and elaboration that would surely touch the fancy of even the most sober-sided individual. Someone in a large hat, for instance, looks "like a snow bird under a sifter," a ne'er-do-well "lacks a dollar and a half of being worth a damn." Someone who hasn't eaten in a while remarks, "It's been so long since I've had any food, my stomach thinks my ribs have taken in washing" or "My stomach called up to see if

108

my throat was slit." But after a good feed, they might be "as full as a frog full of flies" or "so full it makes you poor to carry it." Here is a small sampling from Maryland to which any reader can add ad infinitum.

as easy as pie

as skinny as a bean pole

as dark as the inside of a cow

as ugly as a mud fence

as easy as falling off a log

as big as a house

as happy as a clam at high tide

as dumb as an oyster

as polite as a dog pissing on a briar

as black as sin

as snug as a bug in a rug

as bright as a button

as tight as beeswax

as cold as a well digger's ass

as crazy at Tom Curtz's dog

as pretty as a steamboat

as dark as pitch

as hungry as a bear

as crazy as a loon

as drunk as a skunk

as busy as a cat with diarrhea

as busy as a one-eyed dog in a meat market

as awkward as a breast pin on a hog

as slick as snot and not half so greasy

as crooked as a dog's hind leg

tighter than the wallpaper on the wall

so thin he has to drink muddy water to cast a shadow

so tough he used to go out every morning before breakfast
with a wildcat under each arm looking for chestnut burrs to
wipe his hind end with

He has as much use for that as a hog has for a ruffled shirt.

That's enough to piss off the Good Humor man.

He's got eyes like two holes in a blanket.

busier than a one-armed paper hanger

grinning like a mule eating briars

a beer taller than a drudge boat's mast

mad enough to chew nails and spit bullets

The Wellerism, which gets its name from Sam Weller in
Dickens's *Pickwick Papers,* is a much older form of proverbial
expression, though examples of it do appear in Maryland
speech from time to time. The form differs from the regular
proverb since we learn, in effect, who made the remark and
when.

"Every little bit helps," said the wren as she spit in the sea.

"I see," said the blind man to his deaf daughter.

"Everybody to his own liking," said the woman as she
kissed the cow.

"That's punishing her with good words," said the preacher
as he threw the Bible at his wife.

"It all comes back to me now," said the captain as he spit
into the wind.

As Kinsey said, "You're O.K. in my book."

"It won't be long now," said the cat as she backed into the lawnmower.

RIDDLES AND TONGUE TWISTERS

Scholars have traced the riddle back to the very beginnings of literary tradition and since the form is basically oral, riddles doubtless have much earlier roots. They appear in Sanskrit and in Greek tragedy (one thinks of the famous riddle the Sphinx poses to Oedipus), and any Bible reader recalls Samson's riddle set forth in the Book of Judges (14:14):

> Out of the eater came forth meat, and
> Out of the strong came forth sweetness.
>
> (Honeycomb in a lion's carcass.)

Actually, Samson's riddle is what is known as a "neck riddle," that is, a riddle supposedly asked a condemned person by their executioners to avoid the noose. The neck riddle describes a scene known only to the questioner. Fortunately not all riddles are this complex and most of them supply the listener with enough information to reason through the enigma.

Though it is easy to set riddling aside as a children's pastime, there is reason to believe that in Maryland's not-too-distant past riddling sessions occurred among adults as a means of sharpening the wits. Alex Kellam recalled the pastime as he remembered it evenings at the local store on Smith Island when he was a child. Sometimes, he explained, these affairs lead to amusing responses:

> To give you some prelude to what they did on the island, they'd get around this store there, and they would look at the Bible and they would get things to stump each other with, you know. So this guy came in—Mitch Evans, but they called him Will Torg. So he came into the store one time and he said, "I guess I got one that will stump you. Does anyone know how long King Solomon's been dead?"

111

Well, nobody knew, and just about this time this character walked in there. It was Harry Low, and somebody said, "Captain Mitch, ask Harry."

And Captain Mitchell stood up and said, "Harry, do you know?"

"Know what, Captain Mitchell?"

"Do you know how long King Solomon's been dead?"

Harry said, "Well, hell, man, I didn't even know he'd been sick."

The account makes more sense when we realize that there was indeed a man named "King" Solomon Evans who for years tended the lighthouse at the northern end of the island near a spot that to this day bears his name, Solomon's Lump.

Despite some residual examples of the older form of the riddle still active in oral tradition, it is clear that this device, once popular as an amusing educational tool, has given way to the sham riddle or the riddling question best known to children. The moron jokes, for example ("Why did the moron take hay to bed with him? To feed his nightmare."), or the ubiquitous elephant jokes ("Why do elephants drink? To forget.") If riddling in the old-time context may have lapsed, many Marylanders still remember riddles that have come down to them one way or another.

> Old Mother Twitchett had but one eye,
> And a long thread which she let fly;
> And every time she went over a gap,
> She left a little bit of her tail caught in a trap.
>
> (A needle and a thread)

> In marble walls as white as milk,
> Lined with a skin as soft as silk;
> Within a fountain crystal clear
> A golden apple doth appear.
> No doors there are to this stronghold,
> Yet thieves break in and steal the gold.
>
> (An egg)

> Thirty white horses on a white hill,
> Now they tramp, now they champ, now they stand still.
>
> (Teeth)

Little Nancy Etticoat,
In a white petticoat, and a red nose;
The longer she stands,
The shorter she grows.

(Candle)

Out in the meadow is a little red bull,
He eats and he eats but he never gets full.

(Threshing machine)

As round as a coin,
Busy as a bee;
The prettiest little thing,
You ever did see.

(Watch)

What shoemaker makes shoes without leather,
With all four elements put together?
Fire, water, earth, and air;
Every customer has two pair.

(Horse shoer)

A riddle, a riddle, I suppose,
A thousand eyes and never a nose.

(Thimble)

Two lookers, two crookers,
Four hang-downs, one switch-about.
What is it?

(A cow)

Patch upon patch and hole in the middle,
Tell me this riddle and I'll give you a gold fiddle.

(Chimney)

As I was going across London Bridge,
I met old Daddy Gray.
I ate his meat and drank his blood,
And threw his bones away.
Now just who is Daddy Gray?

(An oyster)

As I was going across London Bridge,
I met my sister Ann.

I cut her throat and sucked her blood,
And let her body stand.

(Bottle of whiskey)

Two little brothers,
Both the same burden bear;
The colder the weather,
The hotter the air.

(Andirons)

Over, over, in between,
Heart-shaped tents of shining green;
I spread gray skirts to greet the sun,
Then fold them close, my work is done.

(Morning glory)

Black without, red within,
Pick up your foot and put it in.

(Boot)

I have legs but cannot walk;
A leaf but am no tree;
I may be square or round or long—
Sometimes you sit on me.

(Table)

I have eyes but cannot see,
A skin but not a face;
When farmers dig up ground for me,
They find my hiding place.

(Potato)

What goes all over the house during the day
And sits in a corner at night?

(Broom)

What won't go up the chimney up,
But will go up the chimney down,
And won't go down the chimney up,
But will go down the chimney down?

(Umbrella)

What goes up and downstairs on its head?

(Shoe nail)

114

House full, yard full, and can't catch a cup full.

(Smoke)

We have tongues but never talk,
Some eyes but never see;
You take us with you when you walk,
Now what can such things be?

(Shoes)

I went to the field and got it. I took it home in my hand because I couldn't find it. The more I looked for it, the more it hurt. And when I found it, I threw it away.

(Thorn)

If a dog's front legs are traveling thirty miles an hour, what are his hind legs doing?

(Hauling tail)

What's the best way to make a coat last?

(Make the vest first)

What goes up and never comes down?

(Your age)

What do you cut off at both ends to make longer?

(A ditch)

What is it a poor man puts on the ground that a rich man puts in his pocket?

(Snot)

Most riddle collections contain a section called "the pretended obscene riddle." These riddles call to mind something slightly off-color when in fact the answer is downright innocuous. Here is a sampling from the repertoire of Maryland riddlers:

Belly to belly, arm around the back,
Big lump of fat meat to fill up the crack.

(Mother nursing her child)

Under my apron there's a little round hole,
If you please to believe it's as black as coal.
You can pull it, you can stretch it.
You can do it no harm,
You can put a thing in it as long as your arm.

115

What is it?

> (Woman knitting a black
> stocking with her needles
> and yarn)

It's thin, long, stiff, and slender,
You stick it in and wiggle it about,
And then the juice comes running out.
What is it?

> (An oyster knife)

What's long, slim, and slender, tickles where it's tender and
hurts where the thing goes?

> (Whip)

Like the riddle, the tongue twister entertains adult and child
alike. In some cases the tongue twister has a built-in function.
Besides sheer entertainment, the tricky alliteration of the
tongue twister sometimes makes it almost impossible not to
utter a risque word, but done in the ritual of the verbal exercise
it becomes perfectly acceptable. For instance, if you say quickly,
"I slit a sheet, a sheet I slit; upon a slitted sheet I sit," a scatological term is bound to slip out unless you have remarkable verbal
dexterity. But if you are familiar with the overall process of
tongue twisting, it doesn't really matter. In fact, that seems to
be the point of the activity and simply lends another element of
amusement to the situation. Some Maryland examples:

She sells sea shells; shall he sell sea shells?

Shave a cedar shingle thin.

Frank threw Fred three free throws.

Tillie's twin sweater set.

Fred threads red thread.

A fly and a flea were caught in a flue one day. Said the flea,
"Let's fly," said the fly, "Let's flee." So they flew through the
flaw in the flue.

Sweet Sally Sanders said she saw seven segregated sea
gulls sailing swiftly southward.

Using traditional methods, Herman "Bill" Dixon operated a boat-building shop in Maryland for more than thirty years. (Calvert Marine Museum photograph by Carl Fleischhauer)

He sawed six long, slim, slender, slick saplings.

I'm a fig plucker, I pluck figs. I'm the best darn fig plucker that ever plucked a fig.

A big black buffalo blew bubbles.

An old scold sold a cold coal shovel.

She sits in her slip and sips Schlitz.

Two toads totally tired tried to trot to Tadbury.

Rubber baby buggy bumpers.

Theophilus Thistle, the cross-eyed thistle sifter.

Tongue twisters frequently fuse with riddles as in this convoluted description of someone watching a bear tear up a fence:

As I went up to hazel-dazel,
I looked out the razzle-dazzle;
I saw old mother middlecum-maddlecum
Tearing up my striddlecum-straddlecum.
If I'd had my diddlecum-daddlecum,
I'd have shot old mother middlecum-maddlecum.

Or they become part of a long jingle or a short song:

Sammy was a sailor, a sailor brave and bold;
He shipped aboard a whaler and tumbled overboard.
He shouted, "Someone save me,"
And someone said, "Go hang."
The sharks were swimming madly as the sailors sang:
"Swim Sam, swim Sam, swim Sam,
Show them you're some swimmer;
Swim like Snow White's swans swim,
You know, like Snow White's swans swim.
Six white shimmering sharks are out to get your limbs,
So a swim well swum is a well swum swim,
So swim, Sam, swim Sam, swim Sam."

CHILDREN'S GAMES AND TRADITIONS

Children as we know can be intolerant little creatures when they put their minds to it. They are extremely conservative and quite inflexible when it comes to the way something should be done. Aggravating as it may be for parents at times, this kind of behavior is a great advantage for anyone trying to study traditional games and play patterns. One reason that children's games have persisted in much the same form for hundreds, even thousands of years, is because, when playing, children seem to have a fetish for "doing it right." If you don't play the game according to the homegrown rules of that particular playground, you get ostracized by the group, and if there's one thing most children can't stand, it's being left out.

Anyone curious about the persistence of children's games need only go back and take a look at Lady Gomme's two-volume work, *The Traditional Games of England, Scotland and Ireland* (1894 and 1898) or W. W. Newell's pioneering study in this country, *Games and Songs of American Children*, to see just how little these games have changed in the last eighty to ninety years. Curiously enough, these early scholars thought they were gathering the last residue of a dying tradition. To change that view, all we would have to do is take Gomme or Newell into a Baltimore schoolyard at recess on a nice April day. What they would see would no doubt astonish them.

Children's games occur in incredible variety. Considering only a few types in Maryland, we find chasing games, guessing games, forfeit games, ball games, hiding games, jumping and hopping games. Some of these games are frequently accompanied with rhymes, jingles, or chants, and one thinks here, for example, of the abundant lyrics that accompany jumping rope. Anyone who has watched while two adept rope turners and a jumper wind through the intricacies of "Charlie Chaplin Went to France" or "Cinderella Dressed in Yellow" can see why these games play a vital part in developing a child's verbal as well as physical dexterity.

Sampling children's games in Maryland, one is struck by the similarity of the games as played in different parts of the

119

state. What seems to alter more than the game itself is the name, and some of these have an imaginative ring to them: "Buttons on the Steps," "Beast, Bird, or Fish," "I'm Going to Jerusalem," "Fox in the Morning," "Ghost in the Graveyard," "Candy Kisses Game," "My Father Owns a Grocery Store." Other games from a variety of informants, both adults and children, include:

Donna Died

There is a circle game, with one girl in the middle. She stands and goes through motions or answers the questions that the girls in the outside of the circle ask. They chant, "Donna died. How did she die?" The girl in the center shows this answer by going through some action. She acts out the answer. The girls in the outer ring ask: "Where did she live?" The girl answers, "Tennessee."

The group says: "Wear their dresses up above their knees," and the girls all pull their dresses up above the knee.

The girl in the middle circles and points to another in the outer ring. Then everybody chants this rhyme:

> She never went to college;
> She never went to school.
> We all found out
> She's an educated fool.

Then the girl who was pointed at goes into the middle and the whole thing starts over again.

Red Light Green Light

One child is chosen to be the leader who calls, "Red light." He stands some distance from the other children while they remain at the starting line. While he is counting to ten with his back to the other children they run forward to reach him and tag him. However, when he calls, "Red light," all the children must stop and not move. If he catches anyone moving they are out of the game. If anyone gets to tag him before he finishes counting and before he says, "Red light," that child is the leader for the next game.

Giant Steps

One person is chosen to be "mother" and stands a few feet in front of the rest of the players behind a line. The "mother" tells each person, in turn, a certain kind and number of steps to take and, before doing this, the player must say, "Mother, may I?" Failure to do this means the player must go back to the line and start over again. The first person to reach "mother" is the new leader. Some of the steps that "mother" would use were the following: scissor steps, umbrella steps, giant steps, baby steps, and elephant steps. The "mother" could make up new steps and name them herself, so long as she demonstrated them.

Button, Button, Who's Got the Button?

A button or some other small object was used to play this game. The players either stood or were seated in a line and one person had a button. With the button in his hand, the leader gave each person a chance to guess which hand it was in. If he missed, he was eliminated from the game. The last person in the game was the next leader.

I played this game while attending the Dickerson Elementary School in Dickerson, Maryland. The children who played it ranged from six to twelve years of age.

Huckle Buckle Beanstalk

An object is shown to all the children. Then three children are picked to leave the room. One child takes the object and hides it. It must be in sight but must also be hard to find. The three children return to the room and look for the object. The first child spots it and says, "Huckle buckle beanstalk," and goes and sits down. The other children try to find it and when they do they say the same thing. The child who sees the object first gets to be the one to hide it the next time.

Fox and Geese

Outdoors, draw a large wheel with spokes. Choose one person to be the fox. The rest of the kids are the geese. At the word "Go," the fox chases the geese through the spokes and the rim of the wheel without touching the spaces in between or the space outside the wheel. The goose who is caught then becomes the fox, and the game begins again.

Swinging Statues

One kid was the swinger. He swung the other kids around and let go of them and they were supposed to freeze in a certain position and not move. If they moved they were disqualified. The swinger chose the best-looking position and picked one, and that kid got to be the swinger the next time.

Upset the Fruit Basket

The players sit around in a circle. Each player is given a name that is the name of a fruit. The names are divided into pairs, that is, two people to the same fruit. An extra person is placed in the center of the circle. She calls a fruit and the two people who are that fruit try and exchange seats. Meanwhile, the girl in the middle tries to get one of the seats. The person left over then becomes the leader. If the person in the middle does not get the seat away, she assumes the name of that fruit. The person in the middle may call, "Upset the fruit basket," and then everyone changes seats and again the person left over is the leader. My friends used to play this in elementary school in Frederick, Maryland.

Ruth and Jacob

This game is a version of "Blind Man's Bluff." The person chosen to be IT is blindfolded. The other players walk around within a set boundary. The blindfolded person calls, "Ruth," and the others answer, "Jacob." The game continues in this manner until someone is caught. When someone is caught the person who is IT must identify whoever he has caught. Then the person caught becomes the IT. I used to play this game in Beltsville, Maryland, when I was about ten years old.

Punch and 'Nella [Punchinello]

This game has a rhyme to it.

> Look who's here,
> Punch and 'nella funny fella,
> Look who's here
> Punch and 'nella funny you.

> What can you do,
> Punch and 'nella funny fella?
> What can you do,
> Punch and 'nella funny you?

> We can do it too,
> Punch and 'nella funny fella
> We can do it too,
> Punch and 'nella funny you.

> Who do you choose?
> Punch and 'nella funny fella?
> Who do you choose?
> Punch and 'nella funny you?

One player is Punch and the others form a circle around him. The first verse of the rhyme has no actions. During the second verse Punch does some simple actions and the others join in the third verse. On the fourth verse Punch closes his eyes and turns in a circle while the others turn in the opposite direction. At the end of the fourth verse, everyone stops and the person at whom Punch is pointing is the next Punch. The game is usually played by children about six years old.

Rhymes appear in other types of children's play lore as well, for instance, when they count out to find who will be IT for the game or who will be the rope turner for jump rope. "I lit a match and put it O-U-T," says one of the group members, pointing variously at different people. When their finger falls on the person who corresponds with the T in OUT, that person is selected or eliminated depending on the format. Most counting out formulas are done in rhyme.

123

1-2-3-4
Mary at the cottage door,
5-6-7-8
Eating cherries off a plate.
O-U-T spells OUT.

Fish, fish,
In the dish,
How many fishes
Do you wish?

Out goes the rat,
Out goes the cat,
Out goes the lad
With the seesaw hat.
O-U-T spells OUT.
So you go out.

Though rhymes such as these appear constantly in many children's games the world over, none seem quite so imaginative and catchy as those chanted while children jump rope. Here is a profusion of names, places, characters, objects, and wild non sequitur situations that could only issue from the fanciful mind of a child. In Kensington, Maryland, for example, the rope begins to turn, a child steps in to perform, and this rhyme picks up:

Winstons taste good, like a cigarette should,
Winstons taste good, like oompa oompa,
Want a piece of meat?
Pie too sweet, want a piece of meat?
Meat too tough, want to ride a bus?
Bus too full, want to ride a bull?
Bull too black, want to ride a Cadillac?
Cadillac too new, want to ride a gnu?
Gnu too big, want to pick some figs?

(Jumper keeps going until he misses or fails to make up a new rhyme.)

Teddybear, teddybear, touch the ground,
Teddybear, teddybear, turn around,

124

Teddybear, teddybear, jump up and down,
Teddybear, teddybear, get out of town.

Not last night but the night before,
Twenty-four robbers knocking at my door.
As I awoke I found this note,
And this is what it said to me:
"Spanish dancer, give a high kick,
Spanish dancer, turn around,
Spanish dancer, touch the ground,
Spanish dancer, get out of town."

I'm a little Dutch girl dressed in blue,
These are the actions that I can do:
Salute to the captain,
Curtsy to the queen,
Touch the bottom of the submarine.
If you touch it ten more times,
You may get your turn again.

Down in the valley where the green grass grows,
There sat Julie as sweet as a rose.
She sang, she sang, she sang so sweet,
Along came Bill and kissed her on the cheek.
How many kisses did she receive?
(Jumper jumps until she misses.)

From Easton, Maryland:
        Johnny over the ocean,
        Johnny over the sea,
        Johnny broke the milk bottle—
        Blamed it on me.

        I told my brother,
        Brother told sister,
        Sister told mother,
        Mother told father.

Father gave Johnny
Some RED HOT PEPPER!

From the streets and playgrounds of Baltimore:
I wish I had a nickel,
I wish I had a dime,
I wish I had a boyfriend,
To love me all the time.

My mother gave me a nickel,
My father gave me a dime,
My sister gave me a boyfriend,
To kiss me all the time.

My mother took my nickel,
My father took my dime,
My sister took my boyfriend,
And gave me Frankenstein.

He made me wash the dishes,
He made me wash the floor,
He made me so disgusted,
I kicked him out the door.

Miss Lucy had a baby,
She called him Tiny Tim;
She put him in the bathtub,
To see if he could swim.

He drank up all the water,
He ate up all the soap;
He tried to eat the bathtub,
But it wouldn't go down his throat.

Miss Lucy called the doctor,
Miss Lucy called the nurse,
Miss Lucy called the lady,
With the alligator purse.

Out came the water,
Out came the soap.
Out came the bathtub,
That wouldn't go down his throat.

Fudge, fudge, call the judge,
Mama's got a newborn baby.
It's not a boy, it's not a girl,
It's just a newborn baby.

Wrap him up in tissue paper,
Send him down the elevator.
First floor—miss
Second floor—miss
Third floor—miss.

Send for the doctor,
Send for the nurse,
Send for the lady,
With the alligator purse.

"Mumps," said the doctor,
"Measles," said the nurse,
"Dead," said the lady,
With the alligator purse.

Cinderella,
Dressed in yellow,
Went downtown
To see her fellow.

She made a mistake
And kissed a snake.
How many doctors did it take?
One, two, three, four . . .

When the sun shines through the leaves of the apple
        tree,

When the sun makes shadows on the leaves of the
    apple tree,
Then I pass, on the grass,
From my leaf to another,
From one leaf to its brother.
Tip-toe, here I go;
Tip-toe, here I go.
  (Jump till you miss.)

Charlie Chaplin went to France,
To teach the girls the hula dance;
A heel, a toe, around we go.
Salute to the captain,
Bow to the queen,
Touch the bottom of the submarine.

Apple on a stick,
Make me sick,
Make my heart go forty-six.
Not because it's dirty,
Not because it's clean,
Not because the kissy boy behind the magazine.

George Washington never told a lie,
He went round and stole a cherry pie.
How many cherries was in the pie?
One, two, three, . . .

Another form of verbal communication occurs in autograph verses, those short squirts of doggerel and poetry that get penned into autograph books or among the pictures of a high school yearbook. Here, of course, folklore has moved over into a written form—which it can do if and when we are able to establish both tradition and variation in the process. In many ways, autograph verse resembles a much more widely used form of written folklore, namely graffiti, the scratchings on walls that comment (often pithily and obscenely) on human events. Behind both forms lies the notion that an individual is setting down something that may withstand the tug of time better than he or she will. As a well-known graffito has it, "Rose was here,/ And now she's gone,/ But left her name/ To carry on." An unknown writer struck a similar note in a Maryland autograph book:

O remember me by the looks I make,
O remember me by your gum I take,
O remember me by the way I walk,
O remember me by the way I talk,
O remember me by my name,
For I write it now in your book of fame.

For the most part, though, autograph book verse, unlike graffiti, gets signed. The following examples all were, but I have left them off here since the names mean little to the reader.

When you get old
And think you're sweet,
Take off your socks and smell your feet.

2 sweet
2 be
4 gotten.

I take me pen,
I take me ink;
Me scratch me head,
And then me think.
Me think, me think,
Me think in vain;
Me think me better sign me name.

Roses are red,
Violets are blue;
A face like yours
Belongs in a zoo.

Boys are bad,
Beds are worse,
Sleep alone,
Safety first.

129

ICURAQT
INVU

I know a girl in the city,
I know a girl in the town;
I'm the girl who spoiled your book
By writing upside down.

First comes love,
Then comes marriage;
Then comes Irma
With a baby carriage.

I wish you luck,
I wish you joy,
I wish you first a baby boy,
And when his hair begins to curl,
I wish you then a baby girl.
And when you start to use pins,
I wish you then a pair of twins.

Love many, trust few—
Always paddle your own canoe.

While sliding down the bannister of life,
Think of me as a splinter in your career.

Roses are red
Violets are black;
You'd look better with a knife in your back.

When you get married and buy a Ford,
Save me room on the running board.

Yours till America gets Hungary and eats Turkey.

FOLK BELIEF

Folk belief and superstition occur in much of what the scholars deal with when they discuss folklore. Belief is a kind of common denominator, appearing in many genres. If you study folk songs and ballads it is there; if you examine folktales, it is there. And folk belief makes itself known in riddles, in rhymes, in proverbs, in children's games as well. What is strange about folk belief is that it carries with it very negative connotations. People who believe in that sort of thing, the line of thought goes, indulge in false logic, unfounded reasoning, ignorance. Yet I would venture a guess there are few among us who haven't at some point knocked on wood, skirted a ladder set against a wall, picked a penny up, worn a special color of clothing on a certain day. Luck is what we're after, and whether we know it or not, we each have our own personal belief system and sometimes go to great lengths to ensure our good fortune. Yet, there aren't too many of us who in this age of science and technology would ever actually admit to being "superstitious."

I remember while collecting folklore down in Crisfield in the late 1960s, I was given the name of a woman reputedly quite knowledgeable in folk belief. When I went to visit her, she was more than willing to talk to me, but she wanted me to know one thing for certain: She herself was not the least bit superstitious. "Fine," I said, and began something like, "Now I've heard some people say that when you hear an owl hoot, that's a sign of death." "Oh," she said, "that's true," and she proceeded to tell me that for several years a particular owl had come and hooted in a tree right outside her window (and she took me to the window and showed me the tree), and every time that happened someone in her family had died. But there was no way I could ever have convinced that woman—nor would I ever have wanted to—that she was superstitious.

Anyone who has observed belief patterns for any length of time realizes that what they believe tends to reinforce itself when events coincide in a certain way. At some point this Crisfield woman may well have had a death occur in her family after an owl hooted in the tree outside her window. Consequently, what had been a lingering belief she had known now became "true." I've had the same experience but under different circumstances.

Years ago when I was cutting my teeth as a young sailor, I shipped as cook on a sailing yacht in the Newport to Bermuda race. Three days out, we were in the middle of the Gulf Stream, had a fair wind and spectacular weather, and every sail was set and pulling us toward Bermuda. I stood on the foredeck whistling away. That was bad luck, the mate told me, very bad luck to whistle aboard a sailing vessel. I apologized. Twenty minutes later, the steering cable parted. Down came all the sails and we lay there and wallowed in the Gulf Stream while another crew member crawled up into the lazarette and for two hours wrestled with the repairs. To this day I have never whistled aboard a sailboat, and, believe you me, no one ever whistles aboard mine.

Folklorists invariably want to discover the context in which folk belief registers; that is, is it something a person simply remembers someone telling them, or is it something they believe implicitly. You get a sense of skepticism, for example, in this conversation I once had with a Tangier Island waterman:

"Captain, have you ever heard about something they call 'buying the wind' around here?"

"Yes, I've heard people say if you throw a penny overboard there'd come a breeze. I don't know if it really works."

"Have you ever tried it?"

"Yeah, I done it once over here in Pocomoke Sound and there come a nice little breeze, but that didn't have anything to do with that."

If we all possess a belief system in one way or another, what then is a truly superstitious person? In the Maryland communities where I have worked, the local inhabitants think a superstitous person is someone who lets belief control his or her life. For instance Eva Dillsworth of Salisbury believed it was bad luck to have a woman be the first to visit you on the first of the year:

> One New Year's Day, Eva Dillsworth's mother called to ask my cousin Ann to tell Eva that she had finished some sewing for her. Ann walked over to deliver the message right away. Eva listened to what she had to say, but followed Ann out of the house. Then she broke off a cedar branch and swept the ground behind Ann right to her doorstep. And when she left she said, "Now the bad luck will come to your house, not mine."

A Mardela man on the other hand had trouble dealing with Fridays:

> I've known John to go out on a Thursday afternoon and plant two rows of corn so he wouldn't have to be starting something new when he planted the field next day. You know it's bad luck to start anything new on a Friday. And if that happened to be the 13th, he just messes around and won't do much of anything.

As folklorist Alan Dundes has pointed out, most superstitions contain either a sign and result or a cause and result. "If you see a falling star (sign), a loved one will die (result)." "If hens roll in the dust (sign), bad weather's going to come soon (result)." Or for cause and result: "To hang a tea towel on the doorknob (cause), is the sure sign of death (result)." "When two look in the mirror at the same time (cause), the younger will die (result)." Magic begins to creep into folk belief when we see the attempt to convert the bad luck of cause and result into good luck. "If you spill salt (cause), you will get a beating (result), unless you throw some of it over your shoulder (conversion)." When a black cat crosses your path, several conversions will reverse the bad luck: "go back, sit down, and cross your legs six times before going on"; "turn around three times to break the spell"; "spit in a hat."

Although most collections of folk belief are lists, the folk themselves seldom sit around and simply catalog superstitions unless, of course, a folklorist asks them to do so. More often than not, a belief surfaces in a little anecdote or tale. People commonly believe, for instance, that the fetus can be marked in the womb if the mother-to-be makes light of an afflicted person or she sees something that startles her. Yet in everyday conversation, the belief becomes imbedded in a factual account, as these two stories illustrate:

> Now there was a woman around here and she had a peculiar, ugly laugh. Oh, it was frightful. You know, you've seen people that way. It was really a frightful sight to look at her when she laughed. Well, this man who used to be the storekeeper over here—he's dead now eight or ten years—when his mother was pregnant, his father laughed and made fun of this other woman who was frightful to look at, and when that child was born—it was a male child—it used to cover up its mouth with its hand, like that. It was exactly like the laugh of the woman they'd made fun of. You could put those two beside one another and if they laughed, they looked exactly alike. Now that's a fact.

> One day during the spring of the year while my mother was pregnant, she had to work in the field planting sweet potatoes. My mother looked up and saw an old woman working in the patch. Her eyes were filled with infection. She said that infection was just dripping from them. My mother got so sick she vomited. And when I was born, my eyes were weak and sore, and every spring my eyelids became infected when I was young. Mother always said it was a birthmark because she had seen that old woman.

Along this same line, I remember a number of years ago when I was teaching a folklore class at the University of Maryland in College Park. In discussing superstition, a woman in the class told this story: Her grandmother had been born with a veil, a thin membrane of skin which hangs over the face at birth and supposedly gives a person special powers, usually second sight. The woman had been living in Baltimore at the time, and to make these powers work for her, she attached the veil to the back of the dresser mirror in her bedroom. That way, when she looked into the mirror she could see the future rising behind her. At one point the family had the bedroom painted and a crew of workers came in to do the job. When they left, the veil was gone. The grandmother always believed that the workmen had stolen it and, knowing how valuable such possessions were to sailors, had taken it down to the Baltimore waterfront where they probably sold it for fifty dollars—a lot of money in 1910.

In this anecdote the folklorist sees several belief systems at work. In the home, the grandmother uses the veil to witness the future and forecast any ill that might befall the family. And as for the maritime side of the belief it is well known that sailors will pay big money to have a veil in their possession since they believe if they have it with them at sea they cannot possibly drown.

In the human life cycle folk beliefs actually start even before pregnancy with love and courtship and then they move on to cover marriage, conception, pregnancy, birth, life pursuits, death, burial, and return from the dead. The full scope of folk belief in Maryland is only hinted at in this random collection from throughout the state.

Love, Courtship and Marriage

The number of white spots on your fingernails indicates the number of boyfriends you have.

If you give a knife to your sweetheart it will cut the love in two.

If you burn a match and it breaks, your love is not true, but if the match burns to the end, your love is true and coming from the direction the match points.

Put a snail in a tray of soft sand and he will spell out the initials of your husband-to-be.

Put a wishbone over the doorway and the first man to come through under it will be the man you will marry.

From LaVale, Maryland:

When I was a young girl a popular thing with the young girls was the "dumb supper." This took place at midnight and was served entirely backwards. At midnight your future husband was supposed to appear at the head of the table. One night my sister and I decided to attend one of these suppers. We had prepared everything and just as the clock struck twelve, the wind began to howl and all the cows ran from the hills and gathered around the house and then there was a shattering noise like chains hitting the doorsteps and my sister and I ran frightened to bed and never stayed to see our future husbands appear.

From the Eastern Shore:

Boil an egg and fill it with pepper. Set a place at the table and put it there. Open the door and turn the lights down low and at midnight the wind will blow and the man who comes in and eats the egg will be your husband.

Reach for the doorknob at the wrong side of the door and you won't get married that year.

If you wet the front of your dress while washing the dishes, you'll marry a drunkard.

If you eat the last piece of food on your plate, you'll be an old maid.

A fifty-cent piece in a bride's shoe insures prosperity in marriage.

If your eyebrows grow together when you're a teenager, you've already met the man you'll marry.

If you wear someone else's wedding or engagement ring, you'll never marry.

If you dream of death, a wedding will take place in the family.

Change the name and not the letter,
Is a change for the worse and not the better.

Birth, Infancy, and Childhood

If a new baby is put on the bed of a married woman who is trying to conceive, she will become pregnant.

If you dream of fresh fish, someone in the house is pregnant.

If your apron becomes untied, you'll soon have something to fill it out with.

If a pregnant woman is shaped round, the baby will be a boy; if she looks pointed, it will be a girl.

If a pregnant woman has a craving for some kind of food and doesn't get it, her baby will be marked with that food.

A pregnant woman should place a knife under the bed as that is good for cutting the pains.

If you don't bite a baby's fingernails off when they get long, he'll steal when he gets older.

Don't let a baby see himself in the mirror or he'll cut his teeth hard.

Put a bottle, a Bible, and a piece of money in front of a baby. If he touches the Bible first, he will become a preacher; if he touches the money first, he will become a banker; if he touches the bottle first, he will become a drunkard.

If you rock an empty baby cart, you'll give the baby colic.

When an infant loses the navel cord, it must be burned; if you throw it away, the child will wet his bed as he grows older.

The seventh child, born on the seventh day, can see visions.

A baby born with a veil of afterbirth over its face will grow up to be a prophet.

If you tickle a baby's feet, it will cause him to stammer.

Home Pursuits

If you put your clothing on inside out, it's bad luck to change it.

If the hem of your dress turns up, spit on it and you'll receive a new one.

If your nose itches, a stranger is coming.

137

If you drop a knife, a man is coming; if you drop a fork, a woman is coming.

For good luck, always stir the cake batter in the same direction.

A visitor must always go out the same entrance he came in.

When you leave home, it's bad luck to go back for something you forgot.

If your ear burns, someone is talking about you.

It's bad luck to give an empty pocketbook.

> See a pin, pick it up,
> All day you'll have good luck.
> See a pin, let it lay,
> Bad luck will come all the day.

It's bad to sew on Sunday; if you do you'll have to pull every stitch out with your nose when you die.

When someone is sewing a button onto a piece of cloth while wearing it, chew on a piece of thread or place the tip end of the collar of your dress in your mouth and chew on it to keep from sewing up your sense.

Never iron your husband's shirttails or else he will be cross.

Make soap on the increase of the moon; it will thicken better.

If you sing before breakfast, you'll cry before dark.

It's bad luck to put a loaf of bread upside down.

If you sweep the floor after six P.M., don't pick up the dirt. Leave it until morning or you'll have bad luck.

If a broom hits you while someone's sweeping, it's a sign you'll go to jail.

Death

If a dog howls, it's a sign of death.

Herman Dixon shares boatbuilding experiences gained since the
1940s. In the foreground are bow stem patterns used in his work.
(Calvert Marine Museum photograph by Carl Fleischhauer)

If a rooster crows on the back doorstep once, company is coming; if he crows three times, death will come to someone in the house.

A blackbird on the windowsill means death.

If a bird flies into the house, it's a sign of death.

Dropping food from your mouth while eating is a sign of death.

If you rock an empty rocking chair, someone in the house will die.

If you hear a screech owl, there will be a death in the family; but if you tie a knot in the corner of your bedsheet, the death will be averted.

If you have a mole on the heel of your left foot, you will die young.

If you accidentally skip a row while planting seed, there will be a death in the family before the crop is harvested.

If a tree or shrub blooms out of season, it's a sign of death in the family.

If there's a death in your family and you don't rap on each beehive, all the bees will leave.

Don't count the cars in a funeral procession or someone else will die.

A green Christmas means a fat graveyard in the spring.

Animals, Animal Husbandry, and Planting

If you have varmints in your house, catch seven and pin them over your back door. Whoever goes out the back door first takes all the varmints with him and you are rid of them for good.

If a pig's tail turns to the right, it's safe for breeding; if it turns to the left, it's not.

To be sure eggs will hatch, put nails under the pine shats in the nest.

A cat that rests on a baby will steal its breath away.

Cut some hair out of a dog's tail and put it under the house, and he will stay home.

About magpies:

>   See one, that's for sorrow,
>   See two, that's for mirth,
>   See three, that's a wedding,
>   See four, that's a birth
>   See five, that's for silver,
>   See six, that's for gold,
>   See seven, that's for a secret, never to
>   be told.

In order to break the bad luck of a cat crossing in front of you, spit in your hat. My uncle carried an old hat in his car just for that purpose, and I've seen him use it more than once.

If you kill a snake and hang it on the fence, it will rain.

When you cut down a bee tree, always say "eema, eema" and they won't sting you.

If a snapping turtle bites you, it will hang on 'til the sun goes down.

Plant all underground crops on the dark of the moon for a better yield.

Never plant beans when the wind is from the northeast; they will create too much wind after being eaten.

When a whippoorwill hollers in the spring, it's time to plant corn.

If you plant lima beans by the light of a lantern, the crop will be plentiful.

Weather

The weather the last Friday of each month determines the weather for the month to come.

Rain before seven, clear by eleven.

Evening red and morning gray,
Sends the traveler on his way.
Evening gray and morning red,
Sends down rain upon his head.

A rooster that crows when he goes to bed
Will get up next morning with a wet head.

A sunshiny shower
Won't last an hour.

Red sky at night, sailor's delight;
Red sky in the morning, sailors take warning.

When crows flock together,
It's a sign of bad weather.

If a cat passes its paw over its ear, it's a sign of rain.

A high hornets' nest is a sign of deep snow coming.

When you see raindrops hanging on the clothesline, you know it will rain again tomorrow.

It will be a long winter if bands on caterpillars are narrow, leaves are slow to fall, squirrels grow unusually bushy tails, skin of the belly of a catfish is unusually thick, the breastbone of a chicken is long and black.

Onion skin thick and tough,
Coming winter will be rough.
Onion skin very thin,
Mild winter coming in.

When the horns of the moon point down, it will rain.

It will snow if turkeys sit in trees and refuse to come down, cats sit with their backs to the fire, dry leaves rattle in the trees, burning wood drops in the fire, air becomes still and silent.

If the smoke of the chimney floats towards the ground, this is a sign of rain.

The number of stars in the circle around the moon tell the number of days before a storm will come.

If the fog lifts,
The rain will fall;
If the fog descends,
No rain at all.

FOLK MEDICINE

Not many of us enjoy the doctor's office very much. It is a place where we go only when we have to, a place of strange antiseptic odors where efficient women in white quick-step about. The doctor's office is where you get poked and prodded, where you get asked a lot of personal questions that are sometimes hard to answer, where you have to promise to do a lot of things that supposedly will spruce up your hygienic well-being. In a word, it's hard to relax in the doctor's office.

If that's the reaction many of us have who live in an urban/suburban society, and I daresay it is, imagine how people living in an isolated folk community must feel stuck in those same white starchy surroundings. Wouldn't it be much simpler, they might reason, to stay in your own community and visit the local "powwow" or "high woman" as these folk healers in Maryland are sometimes called? The high woman lives just up the road in a house much like your own. You know her personally and you have solid proof from your neighbors that the herbs and subtle magic she's been dispensing for years has worked effectively on children as well as adults. Annie Carter of Perryhawkin was just that kind of healer.

> You could probably describe Annie as a sweet old colored lady who would help anyone she could. She's in her late sixties and a hard worker—one of the best farmhands to pick potatoes, beans, cucumbers, or anything like that.
>
> She lives on her social security check but she can't work in the factory during the summer because of her pension check. She raised seven boys and seven girls and some of them went to college. Everyone thinks she's one of the best people around. And if you have some sort of minor ailment, a skin disease or mild sickness, you can just dial Annie and she'll give you a remedy.

143

In Brunswick, Maryland, the folk healer knew how to "blow the fire out."

> Mrs. Shelton lives up the street from grandmother, and grandmother took me up there to ask her about it. About fourteen years ago, she [Mrs. Shelton] burned her arm. She doesn't remember how for sure, but she thinks it was a coffeepot or something like that. Well, she came running over to the house and she was in such a hurry that she fell up the stairs 'cause the pain was so unbearable. Her arm was all red and swollen, but it wasn't blistered yet. Granddaddy blew the fire out. Within half an hour the pain was gone and she never did get any blisters.
>
> She remembers just how Granddaddy did it too. She described how he took her arm and made the hand motions and blew. I asked her if she heard him say anything while he was doing it and she said that she did but it was under his breath to himself.

In both these instances, the folk healers are obviously known in the community. They are accessible and they are also individuals the local people feel comfortable dealing with. Beyond that, both folk practitioners employ the two basic ingredients that folk healers have used for hundreds of years: natural and magico-religious folk medicine.

Annie Carter's remedies spin off a knowledge of herbs and simples, home remedies that have doubtless been passed along to her either by a relative or someone in the community who possibly recognized in Annie a likely successor. Although her practice has been somewhat updated with the telephone—a kind of "dial a folk remedy" if you will—the curative procedures and products that she uses date well back. In fact, many of the traditional cures used by folk practitioners today were once listed in large pharmacopeias published back in the eighteenth century. With the development of medical science, physicians discarded many of these, but these cures filtered down and became the basis for much of what we term folk medicine today.

In the Brunswick grandfather's cure, on the other hand, we enter into the realm of magic and religion. He uses no potions or herbs to cure the burns, only motions and words, and though the patient remembers only something muttered "under his breath to himself," chances are good that his incantation invoked the deity in one way or another. Whether he knows it or not, this healer is drawing on a tradition that dates back to the Reformation when in Protestant Europe all the formal healing connected with the Catholic church and its saints went underground and became the property of the folk.

One thing you notice very quickly in the study of folk medicine is that the ailments that medical science seems to understand least often have the most folk cures. One thinks of rheumatism, colds, cancer, hiccups, sties, and, of course, most unpredictable of all, warts. There were times with warts when even a bona fide physician deferred to a folk practitioner, as Steve Ward of Crisfield explained:

> There used to be some "doctors" in this area who could cure your warts. There was a time when I had grown this big horn wart on the end of my nose and I went to a regular doctor in the village and he wouldn't touch it. He told me to go see George Stevenson. Said he could fix me up. My regular doctor said all he [Stevenson] used was spit and all he did was rub a little spit around on the wart and it went away. But in the end I didn't go; I went to Baltimore instead and had it burned off.

Healers can at times remove warts by absorbing them onto their own skin. When a huge blood wart appeared on the back of a Mount Vernon man he went to the local high man who simply stared at it. Two days later the patient met the healer at the store, remembered the wart, felt for it, and found it was gone. When another wart arose on his hand he knew exactly where to go. This time the healer took a look at his patient's wart, rolled up his sleeve to reveal an arm totally covered with warts. "I think I've got room for one more," he said and proceeded to stare this wart off as well.

At work here is the process of "transferring" common in much of folk medicine. Somehow, frequently through magic, your warts or your ailment are transferred to either an animal or another person. This can be done by "counting away," for example: "To remove warts cut a hole in a stick for each wart. Throw it away. When someone picks up that stick he'll get your warts." Or by "selling away": "You want to get rid of warts? Just rub a penny over them and throw it over your left shoulder. Don't ever look at that penny again and your warts will go away."

Some people may be surprised that, in the waning decades of the enlightened twentieth century, certain forms of magic still persist. But is it really so surprising? After all, in the recent past we learned that Ronald Reagan, while he was president of the United States, let his wife Nancy's preoccupation with astrology control some of his own comings and goings as head of state. If the president can have a little magic in his life, why not the folk?

Listed below are again but a token offering of the folk remedies that have been observed in the state of Maryland.

For colds, rub the chest with goose grease, make a poultice of crushed onions and put it on the chest, drink kerosene and sugar.

For a cold and a cough, find a wild cherry tree, scrape off the bark; put it in a pot and boil in water. Boil it down to a syrup, add sugar and drink.

For corns, take one teaspoon of pitch, brown sugar, and saltpeter, and simmer together. Pare the corn and place the salve on a soft piece of leather and put over the corn. Remove it in two or three days and the corn will come off with the patch.

To cure a child of whooping cough, take him into an old mine backwards.

To get rid of freckles, wash your face in the dew of the first day of May.

To relieve a sore throat, take off the left stocking and turn it inside out and pin it around your neck.

For fertility, a man should eat sunflower seeds.

If you have a toothache, fill your mouth with water and run around the house three times without thinking about your tooth and it will go away. When this fails, run around one more time and the pain will stop for sure.

If a child has asthma, bore a hole in an upright post, put a piece of the child's hair in the hole and close it with a peg. Do this at sunrise and the asthma will go away.

To cure a child of mumps, rub his jaw on a hog trough. If he's too sick for that, bring the hog in and let him rub his jaw on the animal.

To cure an earache, blow smoke in a person's ear.

When you have a cut that won't stop bleeding, place a piece of thick rye bread on it.

My mother puts lily leaves in whiskey and when we get cut and it bleeds a lot, we wrap the lily leaf on the cut. It stops the bleeding and the cut never gets infected.

To cure athlete's foot, tie a piece of woolen yarn around the toe.

For smelly, sweaty feet, soak them several times in formaldehyde or walk barefooted as often as possible in clay.

A rattlesnake's skin around your foot eases cramps.

If you get a sty in your eye, you got it because you peed in the road. To get rid of it, rub it with an old wedding band.

Should you have a stye in either eye, go to the fork in the road and say to the first person that passes by, "Stye, stye, leave my eye,/Catch the first one that goes by."

To ward off disease and keep from getting the itch, wear an asafetida bag around your neck.

To cure hiccups, blow into a paper bag or sip a glass of water from the opposite side, or put your index finger in your ear and drink a glass of water.

To get rid of warts, take a kernel of corn and crisscross it over the wart nine times. Then feed the corn to a chicken and the wart will go away.

Rub a wart until it bleeds; then rub the bleeding area with a flannel cloth until the bleeding stops; then bury the cloth in the ground, and when it rots the wart will go away.

Tie a knot in the string over a wart and then throw the string into the water. When the string rots, the wart will disappear.

To cure warts, find a hollow stump in the woods with water in it; wash your warts there and they will go away.

Take an old dirty penny, rub it on your warts, and then throw it over the right shoulder facing a full moon, and the warts will go away.

Rub a chicken liver over a wart; then put the liver in a holly tree in the woods and the wart will go away.

To cleanse the system, take a teaspoon of molasses and sulphur every morning in February 'til the sap rises. This is the best spring tonic I know.

A good shot of whiskey will cure anything from ingrown toenails to consumption.

6. Material Culture

FOLKLIFE

WHAT WE have explored so far by way of Maryland's folklore has been the orally transmitted lore, what scholars sometimes refer to as "mentifacts." But there is another entire complex of tradition in the state which until recently has gone virtually unexamined, and that embodies the study of physical objects or artifacts and folk methods. Though European folklorist have been examining this sort of thing for years—the Germans lump it all under the heading of *volkskunde* or folklife—American scholars have been taking the field seriously only in the last twenty years.

In 1968 Henry Glassie published a seminal work called *Pattern in the Material Folk Culture of the Eastern United States* and all at once American folklorists woke up to the fact that if a song or tale could be passed on in a traditional manner, so could a ladder-back chair, or a fence type, or a style of barn or house type, or a way of catching crabs. These more tangible objects and activities, Glassie pointed out, could be observed and studied to reveal not only their place in the culture but also the "mental intricacies" which their existence reflected.

Glassie distinguished an item as "folk" through its form, construction, and function. Form, he maintained, was most important since that was the aspect of any object least likely to change. Construction, on the other hand, could be much more easily influenced by technological adaptation, and an object's function might easily shift with time.

Any object folk in construction is in itself at least partially folk; an object that was not folk when it was produced cannot become folk

149

by usage or association, and a folk produced object does not lose its folk status when utilized in a non-folk manner. A guitar manufactured in a Kalamazoo factory is not folk even when played by a bluesman from the Mississippi Delta . . . When a family moves from a one-story folk house into a modern two-story house and continues to live only on the ground floor, apportioning the space in the new house the way they did in the old, they are using the house in a traditional way . . . Conversely, when a suburban matron buys a homemade lard bucket at an antique shop and uses it for a planter, its use has no relation to its intended or traditional use, but provided it was traditional and non-popular when produced, it remains a folk bucket no matter how many zinnias she packs into it. (Glassie 1968, 12)

Many seasons back I had the opportunity to do some fieldwork with Henry Glassie in Maryland. We spent some time aboard a skipjack going out of Annapolis and then headed down the Eastern Shore to Deal Island and Crisfield. Poking around the waterfront in Crisfield on a grey March day we stumbled upon what I in my naivete took to be just another typical crab shanty, one of those creekside shacks where the watermen store their gear and use as their workplace when not on the water. This one had been deserted for some time, so Glassie and I took a liberty, pushed through the door, and had a look around.

We hadn't been in there five minutes when he said, "You know what we have here, don't you, George?"

I had absolutely no idea.

"This is a croglofft," he told me and went on to explain that it was a common architectural form along the southwestern coast of England, the very area where many original immigrants to the lower Eastern Shore came from. Clearly some waterman had unconsciously designed the interior of his shanty so that only the main room went all the way to the eaves of the building, while the bedroom and the pantry were enclosed, forming a loft which one could reach by ladder. In the main room the waterman kept a tool bench and the necessary implements for working on his boats and repairing his fishing gear. In the loft he stored actual items he worked the water with: an eel gig for spearing eels, an eelpot made from white oak splits, a live box or tow smack for keeping catches fresh, a set of both oyster tongs and nippers, and a handful of duck decoys. Taken in the full round of a year, these items spelled out season by season one man's time and traditional ways of working on Tangier Sound and Chesapeake Bay.

FOODWAYS

It is these recurring patterns in everyday life that interest students of folklife, and they can confront them head-on when they know what to look for. Food preparation provides as good a place as any to start looking, for all of us do, after all, have to eat. But before you can even begin to work with livestock in the kitchen, you've got to slaughter it. German farmers in western Maryland took care of hogs this way:

> We usually butchered about six hogs a year. They weighed around 200 or 225 pounds and were about a year old. We always did this around Thanksgiving 'cause the meat would keep better in cold weather. Used to shoot the hog between the eyes with a twenty-two and one shot usually did the job. Then we'd slice the artery in the neck and allow all the blood to drain out for several minutes. Then we'd dip them in a large barrel of boiling water and that would scald all the hair and then we'd take a sharp knife and when the body cooled, scrape it clean. Then we let it cool overnight and the next day we cut the body lengthwise and cut off all the parts we needed.

Using a variety of sources, George McDaniel, in his book *Hearth and Home*, pieces together what the next stages in the process were, at least as they occurred among black families in St. Mary's County fifty years ago. The sides, shoulders, and hams were rubbed down with a combination of salt, pepper (sometimes red pepper), and molasses and brown sugar if a sugar-cured ham was desired. The meat then sat on the shelf in the meat house for six or eight weeks before it was suspended from hooks to let the salt run off. Then it was smoked over a slow fire for a few days before being hung for storage.

Though hog meat went into a variety of recipes, one of the oldest and most traditional in St. Mary's County is cabbage-

151

and-kale-stuffed ham. Not well known at present, the recipe has been kept alive at such unlikely places as the Belvedere Motor Inn in Lexington Park, and by individuals like William Taylor who caters special events at Sotterley, the old plantation house in Hollywood. According to Taylor, the tradition of the stuffed ham goes back to slave times when meat was in short supply and the vegetables were used to extend the fare. Early on, the slaves simply mixed the vegetables with the hog jowls after the master had used the ham, but so succulent did the slave concoction prove that the ham itself began to be stuffed and served on the tables of the main house.

As with any folk recipe, there are as many variations as there are cooks but aficionados say the ham that works best is a coarse country ham. Pockets are slit in the ham and into them go a combination of kale and cabbage and celery, if desired. The ham is then seasoned liberally with both black and red pepper and mustard seed. Next the ham goes into a cheesecloth which holds everything together and is boiled, then cooled and sliced for serving. Stuffed ham is always served cold and most traditionally at Christmas and Easter.

Better known as a traditional Maryland recipe are beaten biscuits. "I recommend three Maryland beaten biscuits, with water, for your breakfast," writes John Barth in *The Floating Opera*. "They are as hard as a haul-seiner's conscience and dry as a dredger's tongue, and they sit for hours in your morning stomach like ballast on a tender ship's keel." Hard they are, so hard that many people who have not encountered them before think they have gone stale. But once you get through the tough outer crust, what waits within is well worth the effort.

The ingredients are simple enough: flour, country lard, water, sugar, salt, a smidgen of baking soda. The tradition behind Maryland's beaten biscuits goes back to the early settlers who learned how to prepare them from the Indians, and apparently the secret was to pound the devil out of the dough for twenty-five minutes or more so as to aerate it before it was hand formed into biscuit size and then baked. The biscuits can be eaten with butter or jam or in company with a sugar-cured country ham. Then too, the consistency of the biscuits allows them to be carried in the pocket like hardtack, and eaten whenever the urge arises. According to Ruth Orrell who bakes Maryland beaten biscuits commercially in Wye Mills, the only thing that will wreck a biscuit is mold. Even when they get stone hard with age, they can still be broken up and used to bread a batch of oysters or a pork chop.

Although the stuffed ham and the beaten biscuit appear to be indigenous to the state, a great many Maryland traditional recipes come from one ethnic source or another. Here, for example, is a family recipe for "filled noodles" which a Garrett County woman learned from her German mother:

> First take some celery, about two onions, a little parsley, pepper, and salt, about as much as you think. Stew the onions and celery in a little butter or oleo. Cut up bread (I use about two loaves), and then mix this with the celery and onions. (I never use the crust of the bread.) Over this pour the beaten eggs. Use as many eggs as you need to mix good with the dressing. For a big family take about three pounds of hamburger and fry it a little. Mix the dressing and the hamburger together. (The more meat you use, the better it is.) Make the noodles last. Cut them into squares. Don't let the noodles dry or they can't be folded around the dressing and pinched together. Cook the filled noodles in broth from a soup bone or boiling beef. (I always use about a dollar's worth of meat to cook to get the broth.) Cook the noodles about 15 or 20 minutes or a little longer than the noodle soup. Be sure the broth is boiling when you put the noodles in.

SCREEN PAINTING

One doesn't have to look very hard to find ethnic traditions percolating in a city like Baltimore and they don't necessarily have to do with food. In 1975 I was involved with the Maryland Center for Public Broadcasting helping to make a film on Maryland's folk tradition called "The Folk Way." One of the people we filmed was Richard Oktavec, an artist of Bohemian extraction who painted, not portraits or murals, but screens for the windows and doors on Baltimore row houses. Oktavec, then a man in his early fifties, had learned the art from his father, William, who started the tradition just before World War I.

It all began when the older Oktavec was working for the Eclipse Air Brush Company in Newark, New Jersey. A secretary there complained about men who walked by her office window and whistled. William Oktavec began to experiment with placing a lace curtain on the screen and spray painting over it. Then with a brush he painted a window shade with a tassel on top and a brick wall with a potted plant on the bottom. In effect, Oktavec had created the first painted screen. It worked. You could see out but not in. The secretary was left in peace. Then in 1913, after he had moved to Baltimore, Oktavec installed a painted screen in his corner grocery store at North Collington and Ashland Avenue to shade his produce. Before he knew it he began to get requests for this new artistic form. Not only that, but the popularity of his art spawned a number of artists and dabblers from surrounding ethnic communities who also began to turn out screens in the Oktavec fashion.

The painted screen design that has been most popular and come down through time has been the small red-roofed bungalow set in pastoral surroundings—woods, fleecy clouds, flowers, a pond, some swans. But Baltimore screen painters have on request turned out other subjects such as stately ships, lighthouses, Christ kneeling in prayer, Elvis Presley. Though the tradition is certainly not dead, it has fallen in popularity from the 1930s when as many as 100,000 of these painted screens decorated East Baltimore row houses. There are presently around 3,000, and while it now costs between ten and thirty dollars for a painted screen, in the thirties you could have had one painted for a dollar or two by one of the many artists who wandered the streets looking for commissions.

In the last few years, folklorist Elaine Eff has been hard at work documenting the efforts of these East Baltimore artisans in a doctoral dissertation, and her recent award-winning film, "The Screen Painters," has brought to a different audience a glimpse of this urban phenomenon. The artwork has been carried on largely in these ethnic neighborhoods of East Baltimore, and Johnny Eck, who still lives in the neighborhood where Oktavec opened his shop in 1922, represents this tradition better than most since he learned his art directly from the man who began the tradition.

Eck was born handicapped. He had no legs but he never let this deter him. Early in his life his mother convinced him that though he might not be able to climb a tree, he certainly could draw one and so he began to attend the casual art classes that William Oktavec conducted in his shop during the early 1920s. These were not classes in screen painting, as one might suppose, but in the more conventional methods of oil painting and drawing. Yet Eck preferred the screen art. "It's big," he told Elaine Eff, "and the bigger the picture, the more detail you can put into it and the more you can see. It becomes the third dimension."

Though he could and did from time to time paint the traditional bungalow scenes, he secured many of his ideas from picture clippings taken from calendars, comics, and greeting cards which he stored in a collection of cigar boxes. Eck saw himself as someone who could imbue an otherwise inanimate scene with real life. "If I do an old mill with a boat," he explained, "I make the wheel move. Why, the water's pouring out of the little buckets. It's splashing." And when he does a lighthouse, the lights actually seem to flash.

The secret to effective screen painting is getting the paint onto the screen in such a way that it doesn't clog the small holes. If it does, the painting can be seen from within and the ventilation is reduced. Some inexperienced painters poke out the holes with a pin, but that is frowned upon. The key is in the brush stroke. "It's all in the wrist," says one artist. "You've got to keep the brush moving until all the clogs disappear."

RUG WEAVING

In the western part of the state one finds a craft being practiced that is much older and more eclectic than screen painting. In her book, *Weaving Rag Rugs*, Geraldine Johnson explains:

Western Maryland women are creating and using an item today that links this region back to the nation's pre-Revolutionary domestic roots. Just as their ancestors did, Garrett and Allegany women are weaving rugs for their own use, as well as maintaining a small cottage industry neatly located near the kitchens of their homes. Amish women still use floor covering as Abigail Adams probably did, covering the newer, more colorful strips of handwoven carpet with older strips to protect it from a summertime of abuse by muddy feet and the sun's fading rays. (Johnson 1985, 135)

One of the rug weavers Johnson found in the course of her research (she gave her the pseudonym Ellen) ran her cottage industry out of a small Texaco station on Route 219 near Oakland, Maryland. Out of half of the building, which Ellen converted from two burned out trailers, she ran a small grocery store; the other half contained her rug preparation area. Ellen actually made her rugs in her home one-half mile away, but the gas station became her "little place of business" where customers came to buy the more than four hundred rugs she weaves a year.

By far the longest and most tedious part of the rug weaving process is preparing the rags. It takes a full day of tearing and cutting them into even strips and knotting or looping them into bundles just to make a rug three to four feet long. This Ellen does at the gas station during business hours. From there the process moves to the weaving room situated in part of a onetime chicken coop, a low cement-block building behind her house. The loom she uses, a Union Custom Loom, she acquired in 1946, and her husband helped tailor it to her special needs. It is usually threaded for four dozen rugs, twenty-eight inches wide. Once she starts the weaving process it is very much the same procedure over and over: opening the shed with her feet, using the shuttle, pulling back the beater—about an hour to do a rug, then a half an hour to tie it off.

Like many weavers in the region, Ellen didn't take up her craft until after she was married. She holds a strong affection for the past and an admiration for the way things were done back then: "Oh, them old-timers had the most beautiful quilting you ever looked at." Yet built into her seeming nostalgia was a strong mercenary theme. Her weaving developed as a way to bring in some extra cash, a way that allowed her to have the things she needed, and it became particularly important after her husband died in 1962. Though Ellen continually expressed to Johnson an aesthetic appreciation of what she was creating, it was clear that the monetary side of the venture was always in the back of her mind. "Like so many of us," Johnson writes, "she also believes that selling her craft is one sign of its worth; 'Things must be pretty perfect to sell,' she says, knowing her rugs sell well. While she does not sell to tourists, her location, with its easy access to customers, certainly encourages her to weave for those both inside and outside the community."

BOATBUILDING

Herman "Bill" Dixon builds boats—or he used to build them, at any rate, along St. Patrick's Creek in Abell, Maryland, where he's had a boat shop for more than thirty years. Like so many men who follow the water or hang out around it, Dixon dabbled in other things besides building boats. He fished commercially for a time, and also ran a small business selling and delivering soft-shell clams out of his home there in Abell. But back in 1982 when I first interviewed him he was very discouraged about that endeavor and even more upset about what was happening to the watermen's business generally. As he saw it, everything was—to put it in the watermen's parlance— "playing right out." And it was this factor that was obviously going to govern his boatbuilding activities. Dixon told Paula Johnson in 1983: "If everything's dying out in the waters, who's gonna want a workboat? It's very simple."

However grim Dixon's view of the water business might be, there was no gainsaying the fact that since the late 1940s he had built a variety of workboats, sportfishing vessels, and skiffs from fifteen to forty feet for any of a number of clients, and his reputation as a builder who produced quality boats was well established. Dixon's workboat design reaches back in time and tradition to an earlier prototype, the Potomac River dory boat. This two-masted sailing craft was developed in St. Mary's County in the 1880s and was one of the few distinctive boat types produced on the western shore of Chesapeake Bay. Unlike most Chesapeake Bay workboats, which are V-bottomed and cross planked, the dory was long planked, which made it stronger and sturdier, though in construction more time consuming. It was this long planked style that Dixon adapted for what he called his "Potomac River sliders"—so named because of the way they coursed over the surface of the water—and word began to leak out in watermen's circles that his boats were good boats. In the small boat building business, it's all witness and hearsay. With hull design, says Dixon, watermen

> look to see a boat they like when they're out working the river and the Bay and so forth, and if they see something that kind of catches their eye . . . they'll look it over and ask, "Well, who built your boat? And how's it holding up?" and so forth and if they like what the man tells them they'll seek you out and find you. Most little boatbuilders don't do any advertising or anything. It's just word of mouth, whether you built a good boat or how satisfied someone is who has your boat, that's the way you get most of your customers and most all little boatbuilders are like that.

When Dixon began building boats, he did so simply to make something for himself. Others saw it and liked it and so he began to get orders. He claimed he never liked building a boat on contract, however, because owners always called for more extras and wanted far too many changes, then complained about the cost when the final bills came in. Dixon much preferred to build a boat on speculation and then have someone opt to buy it. And once he became known, he never had a bit of trouble selling any of his designs.

He built his long planked boats out of the traditional material: yellow pine or Douglas fir planking on white oak frames. He used conventional tools for the most part, but he claimed the two modern tools that saved him the most time were the air hammer and the portable electric plane. Dixon fastened his vessels together with either Monel, stainless steel, or galvanized boat nails depending on the buyer's wishes and the size of his pocketbook. By and large Dixon's workboats emerged from a set picture he had in his mind (he never used blueprints), but often a boat's particulars were shaped by the way a man worked the water. Different types of oystering in different areas demanded certain changes in the basic design, as Dixon explained:

> Well, I guess mainly one of the most changes in the width of your washboard and how much decking is on a boat or the most changes are made because if it's a shaft tonger he wants his washboards and decking as wide as he can get it. If he's a patent tonger he wants it on the narrower side and so forth like that and also it depends on where the man is going to use his boat. If he's going to work in that Bay he wants it a little higher sided and if he's going to shave tong he wants to keep it as low sided as he can.

It soon becomes clear to anyone listening to builders or watermen talk about workboats for very long that form and function go hand in hand in boatbuilding as they do in many other folk crafts. Something is good or aesthetically pleasing if it performs well. A vessel that doesn't bring home a good catch or get the waterman where he wants to go quickly and easily, just isn't going to be pleasing to the eye. Bill Dixon's boats obviously performed. Bernard Morgan, who owned the *Eleanora M II*, the last of the slider designs that Dixon built in 1981, claimed he could probably buy back his boat in ten years with the money it was saving him on gas. "She pushes easy," he said, "she's lively on the water," and what was more, "you couldn't build them to look no better."

Bill Dixon clearly exemplifies a man in the community who provided a necessary service. He built boats and he built them well, and he proved the old truism that if you furnish quality goods, people are going to beat a path to your door.

Epilogue

IT MAY BE all well and good for watermen to beat a path to Bill Dixon's door looking for a traditional boat to follow the water in. It's quite another thing for a fancy lady from Baltimore, let us say, to read a folklorist's article about a traditional quilt maker in Westover, Maryland, and then drive down to her house and ask her to make a quilt in this design or that design. Suddenly the traditionality of the folk artist is compromised, and with money dangling in front of her nose, the quilt maker begins to work with patterns other than those learned from her grandmother. She gets new ideas, and those fold their way into her art.

It's not that I'm against new ideas—not at all. It's just that my hypothetical example points up the perpetual dilemma that folklorists constantly face. In our effort to preserve and document traditional culture we often destroy it, for we give it a visibility beyond the immediate community that it never had before—in a book, a film, a museum display—and suddenly this art or way of life, at once so "precious" and easily delineated, becomes public property, prey to anyone, vulnerable. Before long the folk tradition is no longer unsullied; in time it is unrecognizable. This is sad for the tradition and sad for the folklorist, but it's a fact of life.

So what do we do about it? There's not much we can do except realize that older folk traditions constantly give way to new and just as vital ones. The folk process still goes on. People still tell stories, and farmers still mend fences and walls in a time-honored way but with slicker equipment. Not long ago I was teaching folklore in the prison system. I used portions of

160

this book as examples of different types of folklore, reading some of the texts to make my point. After class an inmate who had spent his life outside prison on the city streets came up to me and said, "I've never heard of any of this stuff you're talking about in here." I gave him an article on the folklore of the drug culture to read for next week. Before class that next week he came over to me and handed back the article.

"Now," he said, "I see."

By no means am I implying that what is included in this book has been replaced entirely by the folklore of drug hustlers, real estate sharks, or modern day hipsters. Some of it I know hangs on, but it is changing and reshaping itself to keep up with the times. Folklorists recognize that this more recent material needs to be studied and documented as well, if we are to better understand the values and attitudes of modern folk groups. Whatever the case, I still maintain that we have a lot more to learn from the folklore of any group of people than we ever do from the disposable culture we face every hour of every day in the supermarkets, on the billboards, and flickering at us from that wasteland called television.

Bibliography

BOOKS

Beitzell, Edwin W. *Life on the Potomac River*. Abell, Md.: E. W. Beitzell, 1968.

Brewington, M. V. *Chesapeake Bay Log Canoes and Bugeyes*. Cambridge, Md.: Cornell Maritime Press, 1963.

Brunvand, Jan. *The Choking Doberman: And Other "New" Urban Legends*. New York: W. W. Norton and Company, 1984.

————. *The Mexican Pet: More "New" Urban Legends and Some Old Favorites*. New York: W. W. Norton and Company, 1986.

————. *The Study of American Folklore: An Introduction*. New York: W. W. Norton and Company, 1978.

————. *The Vanishing Hitchhiker: American Urban Legends and Their Meanings*. New York: W. W. Norton and Company, 1981.

Carey, George G. *A Faraway Time and Place: Lore of the Eastern Shore*. Washington: R. B. Luce, 1971.

————. *Maryland Folk Legends and Folk Songs*. Cambridge, Md.: Tidewater Publishers, 1971.

————. *Maryland Folklore and Folklife*. Cambridge, Md.: Tidewater Publishers, 1970.

Coffin, Tristan P., ed. *Our Living Traditions*. New York: Basic Books, 1968.

Dorson, Richard M., ed. *Folklore and Folklife*. Chicago: University of Chicago Press, 1972.

Dundes, Alan, ed. *The Study of Folklore*. Englewood Cliffs, N. J.: Prentice Hall Inc., 1965.

Glassie, Henry. *Pattern in the Material Folk Culture of the Eastern United States*. Philadelphia: University of Pennsylvania Press, 1968.

Gomme, Lady Alice B. *The Traditional Games of England, Scotland and Ireland*. London: D. Nutt, 1894, 1898.

162

Johnson, Geraldine N. *Weaving Rag Rugs: A Woman's Craft in Western Maryland*. Knoxville: University of Tennessee Press, 1985.

Johnson, Paula, ed. *Working the Water*. Charlottesville: The University of Virginia Press, 1988.

Leach, Maria, ed. *Funk & Wagnalls Standard Dictionary of Folklore, Mythology and Legends*. New York: Funk & Wagnalls Company, 1949-50.

McDaniel, George W. *Hearth and Home*. Philadelphia: Temple University Press, 1982.

Newell, W. W. *Games and Songs of American Children*. New York: Harper and Brothers, 1903.

Warner, William W. *Beautiful Swimmers*. Boston: Atlantic Monthly Press, 1976.

Whitney, Annie W., and Bullock, Caroline C. *Folk-lore from Maryland*. Memoirs of the American Folklore Society, Vol. 28, New York, 1925.

ARTICLES

Ayers, B. Drummond, Jr. "Of White Marble Steps and Painted Screens," *New York Times*, June 7, 1988, Sec. A.

Dundes, Alan. "On the Psychology of Legend," In *American Folk Legend: A Symposium*. Los Angeles: University of California Press, 1971.

Eff, Elaine. "Behind Painted Screens." *The Sun Magazine* (September 26, 1982): 30ff.

————. "Screen Painters: Unique Treasures in Our Rowhouse Midst," *The Evening Sun* (Baltimore), June 7, 1988.

Himes, Geoffrey. "Film Displays an Area Art Form," *Towson Times*, June 8, 1988.

Oman, Ann H. "St. Mary's County Cooking: A Tale of Two Centuries." *The Sun* (Baltimore), November 15, 1981, Sec. H.

Phillips, Agnus. "Beaten Biscuits," *Washington Post*, February 4, 1984, Sec. B.

Richman, Phyllis C. "Can Stuffed Ham Avoid Extinction?" *Washington Post*, February 17, 1988, Sec. E.

Smith, Linell. "The Screen Painters," *The Evening Sun* (Baltimore), June 7, 1988.